THE LAST GREAT ADVENTURE

A Novel

Donald E. Webber

Exeter, New Hampshire

May, 2018

CONTENTS

Prologue		Page 3
Part 1	The Adventure	Pages 6-44
Part 2	The Return	Pages 46-80
Part 3	The Last Great Adventure	Pages 82-97
Part 4	The Conspiracy	Pages 99-120
Part 5	Incident at Northfield	Pages 122-148
Epilogue		Page 150
Index		Pages 152-159

THE LAST GREAT ADVENTURE

Prologue

What happens when we die?

The Last Great Adventure addresses that question by bringing together specific issues in science, religion and philosophy for the purpose of understanding the possibility of life i.e. consciousness, after death.

This is a story of how continued advancements in science, notably relativity and quantum mechanics, complement mankind's acceptance of religious beliefs and philosophical theories. It also is a story of where we are going when we die and how we get there.

•

The Great Adventure describes a young woman's experience immediately following her death. It also tells the reader all that made that young woman a success in life.

The Adventure then informs the reader what happens when the young woman returns home from her great adventure.

The young woman, Madison, in one trillionth of a second, a picosecond, answers the question "What happens when we die?" For Madison, the adventure in one trillionth of a second feels like an eternity.

•

Relativity is the study of the force of gravity and the structure of space and time, the universe. Einstein tells us a picosecond of travel through the known universe could equate to an eternity for those of us on earth.

Quantum mechanics is the study of sub-atomic particles, waves/wavelets, some of which are classified as fermions, bosons, quarks, hadrons, and photons. If three fermions make up a quark, could a quark hold Madison's consciousness?

Scaled up quantum superposition [atoms and molecules being in two places at once] may prove consciousness such as Madison's can move to another state.

Madison discovers the answer.

PART ONE

The Adventure

THE LAST GREAT ADVENTURE

Part One
The Adventure

Madison died.

She was a talented, vibrant, caring young woman four years out of college who had dreams and aspirations like all of us. Madison loved science fiction; she dabbled in cosmology for fun; she taught high school math and even considered going to school for a higher degree. She loved life; she loved her family; she especially loved her beagle Guinness.

The vastness of space, infinity, timelessness and the concept of nothingness after death had fascinated her since childhood while knowing the extent of her knowledge rested with her innate capacity to think, to reason and to rationalize. Madison often thought "Why is that the limit of our understanding? There must be something else."

The reality of death hardly entered her mind, which is not unusual for a woman her age, and she only confronted it when an older relative or older family friend died. However, automobile accidents come quickly and sometimes with terrible results, which Madison discovered. But her awareness, her consciousness, did not cease in the car crash. Unknown even to herself, Madison still was thinking. Somehow a part of her still was living.

"I hear people talking. Am I dead, or am I having a near death experience? Is this an out of body experience?" Madison was thinking, for sure.

Meanwhile, she was about to experience the greatest adventure of her life and maybe the last.

•

Madison was a Midwestern girl having been born in Minnesota and raised in a small town southwest of the Twin Cities of Minneapolis and St. Paul. Hers was the kind of childhood a city kid, any millennial would love especially in July and August.

Her summer days began with breakfast and a sprint out the door to meet friends. She would run from house to house, backyard to backyard and into cornfields at the end of the street all the time in sight of parents and neighbors who looked out for each other. There were no fences even for family dogs. The whole crew of kids soon would jump on their bikes and ride to the town's community pool where they would have lunch, swim until bored or maybe sunburned, and then start thinking about ice cream and cold drinks rather than sipping lukewarm water out of the public fountain.

So it was back to the kids' neighborhood biking through wide streets, some dirt roads, big Midwestern skies and newly planted trees everywhere in the housing developments. A brief quiet time at home was followed by dinner and playing outside until dark, staring at the stars and being filled with awe.

"Think there are flying saucers out there? How many stars can I count? I see one; I see one - a falling star!" Madison would say those words every night, all the time wondering why falling stars streak so clearly above her. "Why?" she asked. "What causes that?"

•

Immediately before the accident, Madison had been reading Giulio Tononi, an Italian scientist working in the United States, who has attempted to characterize quantitatively the structure that a system must have in order to be conscious.

Tononi is trying to describe what changes take place when we are awake (conscious) and when we are asleep but not dreaming (unconscious). He calls it the Integrated Information Theory. It is still at a developmental phase.

Carlo Rovelli, author of *Seven Brief Lessons on Physics*, writes "We still have no convincing and established solution to the problem of how our consciousness is formed. But it seems that the fog is beginning to clear."

Rovelli also adds: "Most religions demand the acceptance of some unquestionable truths while scientific thinking is based on the continuous questioning of any truth."

•

The adventure in which Madison found herself was one of speed, lightning fast speed, and she was moving so fast she had trouble accepting that anything could move with this velocity. Not certain how she came to this situation, she could see only a tunnel, which seemed endless, with a pinpoint of light at the far, far end. The trouble was the pinpoint didn't seem to be getting any closer.

She wanted to gasp but found she couldn't breathe, plus she could not feel the mass of air moving past her - or was it air at all? Madison wanted to touch the incredible vessel transporting her, but there was no vessel. That, along with her inability to feel anything at all, walls, ceiling, floor, anything tangible, told her nothing was there. Then she asked herself "Can I really see anything? What am I inside, is it a transparent tube, a cylinder, or a tunnel?"

Madison appealed to her inner senses and found nothing. Furthermore, she wasn't hot; she wasn't cold; she smelled nothing, heard nothing and the worst, she sensed nothing real. "Whoa!" she tried to say. But Madison couldn't find the ability to talk either. "I'm a teacher. I understand science and cosmology; I am part of the physical world. I am neither intoxicated nor under the influence of drugs. I am a mature, sane woman, who wants to know what in the world is happening?"

Madison was an excellent student in high school and college where her grades reflected industry and motivation. But this, this was too much, and absorbing the dynamics of this kind of reality was incredibly difficult.

"Is it possible I have entered what science calls a wormhole, a tunnel?" she wondered. "And, why do I remember a doctor pronouncing me dead?"

•

Grade school through 8th grade was so much fun for Madison. She loved to read and more than benefited from the town's new, state-of-the-art library which she visited weekly.

"Can you imagine?" she would say to her parents. "They must have made the library for me."

Church school even became an important part of Madison's life. Teen age clubs, school dances as well as group trips took her to other towns and cities so very different from hers while introducing her to adventures she could hardly imagine. Madison even found herself in Idaho one summer working on a church sponsored, retirement home rehabilitation project. She took a bus to Idaho - all alone - and had the good fortune to meet a nice kid, kind of a geek with a black leather jacket, but nice nevertheless.

The whole world was opening to Madison, or so she thought.

She was healthy, active and smart. What more could be asked of her? Life was a continual adventure, for sure.

"What are you thinking, Guinness, my little baby dog, my little beagle? Why do we think so differently? There must be a reason. I suppose you can think and reason at some level, little guy. Someday I'll make it a point to find out how and why."

•

Madison never liked reading Socrates, 470-399 BCE, known mostly today for the teaching of the Socratic Method. He wrote of a near death experience captured in the *Collected Dialogues* by Plato, as it may have been a record of Socrates himself having had the experience. In one of the earliest written accounts in western literature, Socrates included a tunnel, or in his case four tunnels, which he called the judgment of life reviews: heavenly meadows for one, hellish canyons another, reincarnation another, and finally a tunnel returning to earth. Madison remembered his experience.

•

Madison found herself twisting, turning and rolling around like a marble rolls in a funnel. But she wasn't twisting; she wasn't turning; she wasn't rolling. Madison was aware of all that this ride provided, but she felt she was an observer and not a participant. "How can this be?" she tried to say. "How can anything be?" Analytically and practically minded, Madison, rightly so, was more than confused.

That pinpoint of light remained distant, and time suddenly was not a factor. She assumed she was in the tunnel for a very short time, whether time could even be measured at this speed. Even asking herself was tricky. "Am I thinking? Am I really here? Am I honestly experiencing all of this? Am I dead or what? This can't be; it just can't be!"

A quick flash of fear overcame her. "Always move towards the conflict." she thought. "Isn't courage taking action in the midst of fear?" she continued. "Someone once told me to act as if everything depended on me, and then pray as if everything depended on God."

And pray she did, but she wasn't very sure to whom or to what she was praying. Madison was in a world other than any she ever had envisioned or about which she could even fantasize. "What could be generating that light up ahead?" She thought with a sense of trepidation. "Please tell me it is good, please"

•

In high school Madison read the classics, studied Latin and took an introduction to philosophy. She read Plato and Socrates but quickly became bored with too much philosophical ruminating, as she called it. "Couldn't these people write in English?" Madison would often that say to her classmates knowing language and communication were different a few thousand years back. Even Shakespeare didn't rate highly with her. "I don't like to struggle to figure out each word and phrase in old English even if it is educational to do so." she would tell her teachers.

Still she was a model student who came to focus on math as her real strength. "I can teach this subject someday, she thought. Furthermore I can verbalize some of these impossible formulas so that students understand them, and I am doing that right now in high school." Madison had become a class officer, a member of the student senate and a student tutor in math by the time she became a junior.

Not without boyfriends, Madison dated the high school basketball captain.

She loved him as she did all her close friends but not with enough passion to attend the same college as he, so off she went to one of the finest private colleges in Minnesota, St. Olaf. Happy to be on her own, away from all she had known and on a new adventure, Madison was driven to do good things and to make a difference in life.

•

Madison's consciousness on this adventure is not unlike abnormal properties of super small stuff, quantum bits or qubits (waves/wavelets) spinning and entangling by telepathy, resulting in instantaneous transmission across light years of distance. Qubits are waves such as the polarization of a single photon. One region of space immediately borrows energy from another region through a medium which doesn't have energy at all - a bridge through space, a vacuum, a wormhole which is anti-gravitational.

Light is made of quanta, the same as photons, bundles of positively charged electromagnetic radiation energy. Only light or other waves that have no intrinsic mass can move at the speed of light in a vacuum such as space. Particles of light, photons, which are moving constantly, have no mass, no rest mass.

Madison could see the sun bend space around itself, and the earth spin because it is racing in a space that inclines, like a marble that rolls in a funnel. She could see the earth spin at 1000 miles per hour while moving 66,000 mph around the sun. The Milky Way Galaxy was moving at 1.4 million mph through the universe relative to the background energy left over from the Big Bang, and the universe was expanding 5-10% every billion years. Madison was seeing it all.

"Expanding to where in billions of years?" Madison was asking herself.

•

Madison was streaking through an environment with which she had no familiarity, and she was moving at an incredible speed which she never could measure. "Can anyone live through this? Can I?" she wondered. Her life seemed to have entered another phase, another dimension almost like that of which dreams were made. "Star Trek did this," she thought. "The Twilight Zone was this," she knew. "But what is this, the Outer Limits?" she had no idea. Amazingly, Madison's thoughts were quite lucid even though she began to feel detached from everything she had known. More than feel, she knew intuitively she was more than detached. She had entered an unknown realm.

Madison also was beginning to think she was losing it. "I seem to be able to think, but I don't have a clue about what is happening to me or why. I seem to be able to talk to myself, but I don't even know about that."

Then Madison began focusing on the light ahead, as small as it was. She could almost feel its warmth, its power, and its meaning. It was a good sensation, fabricated or not, amidst her total confusion. It was the first identifiable good she sensed on this, her journey to … to where?

•

Four younger brothers, a sports enthusiast [sports nut to put it mildly] for a father and a mother who kept it all together as well as anyone could in such a large family was the makeup of Madison's early years. She was the first child, the one who set the rules for the boys, or so she thought. She was the favorite of the grandparents which resulted in a day to day contest with her brothers. She also was an overachiever, something none of the boys felt they could best. The boys were athletes, however, which gave them a measure of success over their sister and absolutely a front row seat in the living room with dad when the big games were on TV. Madison and her mom retreated to the kitchen at that point in the weekend just to stay out of the craziness.

Madison often had to say "Yes, Dad, I'll get some more snacks and beer. Just don't give little Guinness any more chips."

If anything formed Madison's personality and mental toughness, it was her family which she loved. She grew up middle class, understood and appreciated it. She felt she grew up with everything a young girl needed, including sibling rivalry. Importantly, she had a positive outlook on life and always looked for the good in everything. Her life wasn't Roseanne or The Modern Family by any means, but the family worked.

•

Madison was learning more than anyone could have known while on this adventure even though she didn't grasp it completely. "All fundamental particles, waves/wavelets, in nature can be divided into one of two categories, bosons and fermions, which make up everything." She was learning by observing.

"Yes, light is made of quanta or photons. They are packages of energy, bundles of electromagnetic energy. A photon has most of the properties associated with particles, is located in space and possesses energy and momentum. But a photon which is positively charged does not have mass and can travel at the speed of light." She was participating.

"If there is a quantum code for all things, living and dead, then there is an existence after death." She agreed with that conclusion by Dr. Robert Lanza, author of *Biocentrism*. She also felt she was proof of the theory.

•

Madison began to see her past, then the present, then her future. She was entering a dimension unlike anything she had known, and it all was visible in front of her, wherever the front of her might be. "Oh yes, the light is in front." Madison quickly regained her perspective.

It was a long timeline of events that she saw, but what she had understood as time and space was changing somehow. They encompassed her rather than functioning as separate entities she previously could not comprehend, but now she began to understand fully the laws of nature and morality in mathematical language, her strength. She even felt gravity bending time as well as space. Madison was not completely fearful at this point in her adventure, questioning or feeling confused anymore, and she began accepting her journey even though that pinpoint of light, still was so far, far away. She also accepted her fate, the purpose for this adventure, whatever it might be. Madison somehow was beginning to understand the purpose and design of the universe, and she was beginning to think she could account for energy, not just measure it as has been the limit of science.

"This can't be a near death experience. It has to be the conduit through which people who die go to…to where? I don't know."

•

College was a relief for Madison. She was away from home, a home she loved but one she knew she would leave someday. "Oh yes," she would think. "I'm away from the chaos brought on by my four younger brothers who always were taking my space, using my phone and playing sports in the second floor hallway of our home, next to my room, driving me nuts." Madison was on-her-own, finally.

Madison also began to appreciate the concept of time. "Whoa!" she thought. "I am away from home after 18 years; I truly am beginning to see a different life for myself; and I have a distinct history already. I can't wait to see what adventures life has in store for me now, and if it is anything like I am experiencing in college, it will be wonderful."

She found she had to study even harder in college than high school in order to maintain her high grade point. She studied sociology and philosophy including Carl Gustav Jung and Immanuel Kant. The ideas of a collective unconsciousness, human autonomy and the universe as a living system required much thought and discussion, yet all of it did not register with her as did mathematics. Analytical

Madison preferred trusted formulas, answers that could be proven on a blackboard, and a disciplined system rather than conjecture and hypothetical illustrations.

●

Madison's high school science taught her that we see everything in three dimensions - length, width and depth, and we experience everything in one time dimension.

Relativistic physics applies a timeline of the past, the present and the future and uses the three (3) spatial dimensions and a fourth (4) of time.

Stephen Hawking, Madison learned, believes he has the ability to live multiple dimensions: past, present and future.

Einstein proved that time is relative to whomever is observing it at a particular speed. A ball thrown inside a moving airplane certainly is moving faster than a ball thrown on the ground. He also found that space and time are not fixed. The faster one travels and moves through space, the slower one moves through time, as time bends due to differences in gravity and velocity.

Space is the movement of thought, past, present and future. Relativity is the study of the force of gravity and the structure of space and time, the universe.

Madison's adventure was helping her to absorb all of this better than she thought she could.

•

Madison began to realize she was conscious of her presence, as conscious as she ever had been. She remembered studying Carl Jung many years ago when reading his theories regarding synchronicity, coincidences, the paranormal and ESP as being components of energy. "Why think of him now? Then again why not? This is crazy. I thought he was crazy. Maybe I am crazy?" Madison was thinking; she was feeling; she was intuitive; she was sensing what? She didn't know yet. Most important, Madison was not feeling alone in this venture. "Why? Is that Jung's collective unconsciousness? Did he know something that only now in this adventure I am beginning to comprehend?"

Or, Madison thought, was that what Edgar Mitchell, NASA Astronaut meant when on his way home from the moon? He said "The presence of the divinity became palpable, a universe of consciousness, a living system."

"What is the presence of the divine? Madison thought. Is this where I am going, to the presence of the divine, or am I going anywhere?"

"If human consciousness can operate external to the body at remote distances, perhaps it can operate without a body?" Madison remembered Mitchell saying.

"Do I even have a body anymore, and am I dreaming all of this after all?" Madison wondered.

•

Math, algebra, geometry and trig - all were of interest to Madison. But physics, especially theoretical physics involving mathematical abstractions of physical objects to explain natural phenomena, was a bit much for her. "Hans Peter Durr and his quantum states are too much for me. If all I studied were Durr's combining collective unconsciousness, a universe of consciousness and paranormal stuff, my grade point would be destroyed. This is just not my thing at this point in life."

More than that, Madison said to classmates, why are these people so into death? Why do college students have to read into things to understand what can't be proven? One plus one equals two not three, and that is it! Let's stay with the basics, write code for programs and do the math."

Madison was growing impatient with aspects of education for the first time in her life, and she also was becoming opinionated and forceful when necessary. The college experience was working as it should, and Madison was learning to become a questioning adult.

•

Madison wasn't feeling Carl Jung was so crazy anymore now that she was on this adventure. He wrote about forgotten information and repressed memories, ancestral memories, deities and myths about which no one has knowledge, about a higher consciousness and ESP. "It's even simpler than that, she thought, he wrote about thinking, intuition, feeling and sensation. Yes, it's the foundation on which the Myers-Briggs indicator is based. I know that stuff now."

Madison accepted Durr's belief that "Just as a particle writes all of its information on its wave function, the brain is the tangible floppy disk on which we save our data, and this data is then uploaded into the spiritual quantum field. Continuing with the analogy, when we die the body of the physical disk is gone, but our consciousness, or data on the computer, lives on."

"I, Madison, must be the embodiment of that data."

•

    Madison began to become conscious of the presence of her mother…then her father…then one of her brothers. "How can that be?" she asked. Madison hadn't seen the three for some time, but their presence was that of yesterday, today, tomorrow. Or was it? Under normal circumstances Madison felt her head would be spinning by now, but these were not normal circumstances, unless sensing that she was undulating, flexing, curving, and twisting on this adventure was the new normal she was to continue experiencing. Then she tried to recall what she was doing before she found herself in this incredible, so incredible journey which panicked her at times, comforted her at times, and left her almost stunned at times.

    Yesterday became visible. Madison saw herself working; she saw herself laughing with other teachers; she saw herself writing home to her parents. Then she saw herself avoiding a speeding automobile heading directly at her after crossing a median, and she heard a doctor say she was dead. Immediately she saw people at her school looking for her today and her mother in tears opening the letter she wrote only yesterday. She cried out but there was no cry, no response and no contact! "What is today, anyway?" she thought. "Is there any meaning to this, to time? What is happening?"

    Frustration seemed to be setting into Madison's experience. Her emotions were up and down amazingly fast.

•

    Following graduation from college with honors in mathematics, Madison began teaching middle school, grades 6 through 8, rather than immediately pursue an advanced degree. "I need an income having accumulated so much debt these past three years, and I can't ask my family to do more. [Madison graduated in three years rather than the traditional four] Plus one of my brothers is in college now draining my parent's resources beyond reason, and I have no idea how they will finance the other three boys. Oh well, I have plenty of time to make more income once I go after my masters."

    Time was beginning to become a real factor in Madison's life, time to do this, time to do that, yesterday, today and tomorrow. "All of a sudden I am so very aware of time like never before. Maybe I should say conscious of time? It sounds more intellectual. And what about being conscious; what about consciousness? Once I promised Guinness, little Guinness - love that dog - I would try to answer questions about consciousness, both his and mine.

Here is a crazy idea. Maybe God is consciousness, and he shares some of it with people and some of it with animals? That would make for a supreme consciousness into which we somehow connect. What do you think of that assumption, Guinness?"

•

Madison asked why waves and particles are different phenomena? Her answer, a stone is particle-like, the size and shape being the same wherever. Quantum entities like electrons have two identities, waves and particles. Ripples are wave-like, the size and shape depend on the media through which they move. Science tells us waves move through the electromagnetic field of space. Waves undulate, flex, curve, stretch, twist and/ or depress due to the gravitational field of space. Space bends; time warps. The sun bends space around itself due to its gravitational effect because space is matter. Planets circle around the sun, and the earth is falling in its orbit because space curves.

It is a scientific fact that time emerges due to heat. [Thermodynamics] Friction produces heat; therefore, the difference between past and future exists only when there is heat. Heat also moves toward cold and never the opposite.

"Time sits at the center of the tangle of problems raised by the intersection of gravity, quantum mechanics, and thermodynamics. [It is] A tangle of problems where we are still in the dark." Carlo Rovelli

Madison loved Rovelli. She also began accepting that consciousness is captured in a wave or wavelet.

"Three fermions form a quark. That's where consciousness lies." reasoned Madison.

•

Madison is beginning to fantasize. She is beginning to feel a completeness never felt before, a completeness that allows her to feel a part of a universe and universes, a part of creation, a part of a grand design. "Maybe, just maybe, this is what Stephen Hawking is talking about in his Grand Design Theory of a multiverse rather than just a universe?" she thinks. "Right now I really, truly don't know."

Madison sees galaxies, so many galaxies, countless, beautiful, spiral, huge and small. She sees stars, millions, billions, trillions of stars so far apart yet connected. She sees 40 billion planets, not unlike earth and maybe inhabitable, circling stars in the Milky Way alone. The beginning of the universe is still there; the expanding boundary of the universe is still there; gravity waves showing the universe expanding 100 trillion times in less than a second 13.7 billion years ago are still there. Madison sees invisible, parallel universes created by Dark Energy. All of that, including the pinpoint of light to which she is heading, still is there. And everything is expanding, including Madison's consciousness it seems, faster, much faster than the speed of light.

A follower of Deepak Chopra, Madison remembers his comments "Our skin is new every month, our liver every six weeks, and our brain changes its content of carbon, nitrogen, and oxygen about every twelve months. Day after day as we inhale and exhale, we give off what were our cells and take in elements from other organisms to create new cells. All of us are more like a river than anything frozen in time and space."

"Yes we are; yes we are!" Madison wanted to shout.

Madison once read that the Greek philosopher, mathematician and astronomer Thales of Miletus, wrote "Nature follows consistent principles." Madison can see that clearly now.

•

Interest in mathematics soon led to an interest in science and cosmology. Even theoretical physics had its place for Madison. "If there is a supreme consciousness out there somewhere, Guinness, and if there is a collective unconsciousness out there as well, maybe, just maybe there is a network of supreme consciousnesses?" Madison was stepping out of her comfort zone. "Good God, puppy dog, who knows what I am into here? But I do know that it has to be measurable by mathematics."

Madison had begun reading Carlo Rovelli, Stephen Hawking, Neil deGrasse Tyson and Robert Lanza. She tried to organize space mathematically only to find it had been done already and by intellects far superior to anyone she had known.

She began to see consciousness as that which religion called God and what science called energy while the source of both remained an enigma. Madison would sit for hours examining the consistency of nature. She would study the stars and constellations and read logs of astronauts only to find a new spirituality and awe.

Deepak Chopra, who she began to see as a spiritual leader of sorts, made her realize just how much of everything we know is connected.

•

Earlier in her studies, Madison learned that dark energy is anti-gravitational, negative gravity. It is a cosmological constant, negative pressure pushing and driving space apart, creating more space and more dark energy, causing the universe's expansion to accelerate. Seventy percent of the universe is dark energy. In addition to causing the universe's expansion to accelerate, it is flinging space apart.

Dark matter is gravity and exerts gravity while having six times the total gravity of visible matter. It does not absorb, reflect or emit light; and its existence and properties are inferred from dark matter's gravitational effects on visible matter. The gravitational effect pulls matter together. Thus spinning, disc-like, spherical galaxies develop from the push of dark energy and pulling effect of dark matter. We can see less than ½ of 1% of the universe while all stars and galaxies make up 4% of the universe. The rest is dark matter and dark energy.

It was Einstein who developed the accepted view of the gravitational field. The reason objects are drawn to planets is that space-time curves due to gravity. Gravity is seen as a medium and not a force.

Madison also learned that theoretical physics employs mathematical models and abstractions of physical objects to explain natural phenomena.

It was not fantasy, for sure, and Madison had learned that first hand on this adventure.

•

Madison is beginning to visualize the Biblical creation story as a brilliant way to understand creation. In its simplicity, covering only seven days, the story allows her to understand just how modern day science complements the Genesis account. And for Madison, there does not have to be any conflict with science and religion - especially now.

Madison also sees the scientific account of the beginning, a quantum fluctuation. She sees the inflation and the afterglow light pattern which followed. A dark period ensued, and then the first stars appeared. Next galaxies and planets formed while continuously moving further and further away from the beginning, the quantum fluctuation. Madison sees black holes forming from stars burning all their hydrogen, collapsing under their own weight while bending space and time, and emitting radiation. She knew that radiation is called Hawking Radiation. She also sees black holes forming in the middle of all galaxies.

She is looking back in time at a cosmic, microwave background that contains the afterglow of light and radiation 13.7 billion years ago. She sees our universe expanding incredibly in a picosecond and later cooling and becoming less dense as it expanded. The first gases, hydrogen, helium, lithium and beryllium form as the lightest 4 elements in the universe while leaving hydrogen as 90% of the universe. The Belgian priest, Georges Lemaitre, was right in 1920 when he called it the Big Bang. Madison sees that clearly now and begins understanding things, amazing realities, she never understood before.

•

Madison remains one of the few who attended church regularly as a kid and still does as an adult. She never had a team practice on a Sunday morning, a program on TV she was required to watch or parents who did not care about her gaining a foundation in religion. However, there were times when she figured her parents dropped the five kids off at church simply to have some private time at home. "Undoubtedly, true." she reasoned.

Madison happily joined her college, non-denominated church and enjoyed the friendships she made. Later when she commanded a better understanding of math and combined it with her interest in cosmology, she came to the conclusion that there must be a god, a creator, an originator. Madison knew science liked to refer to God as energy, but she preferred to use the word God - even lawmaker.

"Faith, is that what we call it? Sure, why not? Where did I read that one who believes there is a god sometimes is best going back to where she started - be it Catholic, Protestant, Jew, Muslim, Buddhist, Hindu or whatever? There is no definitive answer, I know, but surely there is something out there that started all of this - this being the universe and life as we know it. Why else would so much effort be placed on perpetuating theology? Maybe I am naive, but I don't care. War, money, poverty, disease, power, politics and the Popes all played a role in religion as we know it today, but still, I don't care. Religion provides hope, and we all need it.

And I love the creation stories especially 'Let there be light'. How in the world did someone, maybe Moses, come up with that statement when science - assuming there was something like science - consisted of earth, air, fire and water? How did he have any idea about 'In the beginning'? Either he was a genius the likes of Einstein, or truly he was a prophet, touched by God?"

•

Madison had studied two of the greatest stories ever told, those of creation in *Genesis*. Biblical historians indicate the stories reached their current form, not during the crisis of the Babylonian exile of the Hebrews in the *Old Testament*, but later in the sixth and seventh centuries CE. Mesopotamian mythology and the Babylonian creation myth certainly played an important role in the creation stories, as did the Jahwist in the late sixth or seventh century CE. The Jahwist Story focused on man as the cultivator of his environment and as the moral agent.

Sometime after the Jahwist, the Priestly Story was written, focusing on the entire cosmos, while completing the creation stories as we know them today.

Interestingly, Madison accepted those stories as having stayed with us since the book of *Genesis* was written and revised, and that they are interpreted literally and figuratively even to this day by Christians, Jews and Muslims.

Madison compared the Biblical account to the universe expanding 100 trillion times in less than a second at the time of the Big Bang. It was a faster than light expansion, a picosecond. Cosmologist Doug Neidermeyer at the USMA West Point defines it as a trillionth of a trillionth of a trillionth of a quadrillionth of a second. A picosecond is to one second as one second is to 31,710 years.

"The modern Big Bang Theory is one in which the universe has a finite age and evolved over time through cooling, expansion, and the foundation of structures through gravitational collapse." Stephen Hawking

"In short," writes Carlo Rovelli, "the theory describes a colorful and amazing world where universes explode, space collapses into bottomless holes, time sags and slows near a planet, and the unbound extensions of interstellar space ripple and sway like the surface of the sea."

•

Madison recognized she was having an out-of-body experience. "I have read about these, and I have seen movies about these. It's weird; it's unreal; it's surreal! But it can't be." Then again she didn't know. She couldn't see herself in a room or a place or a time she could look back on as the focal point or a point of origin. "I still do not know where I am or where I am going or whether I am going someplace at all," she tried to say. "And all I know is that I'm not whole; I'm different; everything is different."

Madison knew there were over two hundred billion galaxies that have been estimated to be in our universe. The Hubble telescope projects over a trillion. Each galaxy has billions of stars, and each star has at least one planet circling it. Planet Gliese 832c is the latest to be determined to support life albeit 16 times 5.9 trillion miles away from earth. "Just knowing this makes for an out-of-body experience. I'm lost at this point.

Telepathy, am I doing everything by telepathy? Why? Why now? Oh God, I wish someone were here with me." Again she tried to cry out. Again she felt panic.

"Is my mind really a separate entity from my body? I've never given that much thought, but I'm beginning to accept it. Am I different, or is this what everyone experiences at some point? Is that some point death? What is this all about?"

•

Madison's oldest brother, the second child in the family, managed to do everything the opposite of her. When young, she didn't quite catch-on to his antics, but in high school, her brother's silent antagonism to his sister's success materialized in bad grades, rowdiness, drug use, and obstinacy. He had become somewhat of a disappointment to his formerly non-judgmental and forgiving parents, but knowing of his drug use crossed the line. He was a disappointment to Madison as well, and fortunately he did not attend the same college as she.

"How can I help him? How can I communicate with him when he is high? He was so opinionated when we were together during school and family vacations that talking with him was impossible. Maybe I can do it by telepathy, although that is a joke. Somehow I have to penetrate that thick skull of his. Why is it that people can be so different in a family? Why does he boast he can make his mind separate from his body and see us when not present? Undoubtedly it could be drugs, I suppose? Maybe it's that other stuff I have read about allowing for mental properties not being governed by the laws of math or physics. What it comes down to is that I don't have a clue. Who knows, maybe it's LSD?"

Madison knows one's subconscious mind is a million times more powerful than a conscious mind. She also knows 95% of daily life is controlled by the subconscious mind even to the extent that the subconscious can observe the body's operation and manually control it. In the case of her brother, she is afraid drugs have messed him up too much, and all reasonable efforts to help him aren't welcome whether consciously or unconsciously.

•

In her studies Madison read Immanuel Kant as well as Carl Jung. Kant in particular was very helpful regarding her brother's activities in that Kant believed there was a supreme principal of morality which he referred to as The Categorical Imperative. "An action's status is morally good if it is commanded by God." His moral theory was based on his view of the human being as having a unique capacity for rationality.

Madison tried to apply that principal to her brother with some sense of personal relief that an older sister needs in an attempt to help her troublesome younger sibling.

Then Madison read Joseph J.B. McMillan, a South African Scott, who wrote "Perhaps evil is simply reason in service of human instinct? That is certainly the message of Adam and Eve and the Garden of Eden."

"Very, very helpful." Madison thought.

•

Madison began drifting back in time. She began seeing events that she had no ability to understand while uttering "How can I do that? How can I see that? How can I feel that?" She witnessed relatives of long ago struggling to survive in the harshest of conditions. Madison could see wars, ancient civilizations, earthquakes, floods, births, marriages, happy times, sad times. She could see it all as if it were on a timeline in an old Movietone newsreel. She again heard her grandmother call for her at the vacation home. She smelled her dad's pipe and his favorite Cavendish tobacco. Her mother's perfume lingered about her while little Guinness chewed a bone.

More than seeing, Madison felt deep in herself such empathy and sympathy for everyone's participation in the entire story of life. "Mother, you were so right. We are here by the grace of God; we are here to continue the evolution of 'project humanity'; we are here to help one another through life on earth. The meaning of life can be so simple at times."

"My God," Madison uttered to herself. "Everything I am seeing is real, and it's all happening at once. It's happening right now! Absorbing this much, this fast is scary, almost frightening. Yes, it is mind blowing; and my mind, thank you, is blown."

•

Madison was an optimist. Typically she was happy and ready to do most anything work or fun related. She always loved sitting on the floor with a cup of cocoa looking at old family pictures while listening to stories about how the family came to be in Minnesota. She even felt the pain and hardships generations of her family endured. At times she could swear she could see events that happened and hear the voices of those whose bloodline she shared. "Tell that to someone, and they will lock me up!" Madison laughed to herself. Yet her feelings were strong. "There must be something else going on here in order for me to know I participated in those happenings."

She also became convinced humanity was a project of some entity beyond her comprehension. "Project humanity" she loved to say. Regarding the entity, she hoped it was the good and kind creator her church taught her to trust.

Consciousness became another focus of hers beginning with the time she promised her dog Guinness she would determine why her ability to think, reason and rationalize was different than his. "Of this I'm not certain, but consciousness may have begun when man could identify an object with a word. That must have led to mankind to become aware of himself looking at objects and knowing how to classify them. That has to be consciousness, although some would say it is a constant always having existed. In that sense, consciousness is much like God. Maybe it is God?"

•

Madison knew that Einstein convinced us that space and time are not fixed. They are flexible and dynamic as are other processes of the universe. Space bends; time warps; light is warped by gravitational fields.

The general theory of relativity deals with the force of gravity and the large scale structure of the universe. General relativity also is electrostatic force, movement toward or attraction to a central object. Meanwhile the further from the center of the earth, the slower time moves due to that force.

The four known forces of nature are (1) gravity, which works on everything, (2) electromagnetism, which works only on charged particles and is responsible for all chemistry, (3) weak nuclear force, which causes radioactivity, and (4) strong nuclear force, which holds protons and neutrons inside the nucleus of an atom.

Madison also read and questioned Stephen Hawking's comment "The concept of time had no meaning before the beginning." She truly did not know how that could be but was beginning to understand while on this adventure.

•

"Wait! Wait!" Madison shouted without any success. "Hey, anyone, anyone at all, isn't it about time I figured out where I am and where am I going? I feel like I have been in this 'thing' forever; I have been to the center of the galaxy; and I have seen and almost touched Sagittarius and Scorpio. I have been zooming through space at kilo light year speed or faster, whatever that is, and still I do not have any concrete answers. I don't even know why I know what I know about all of this, but I just do. And I have seen the collapsed cores of two neutron stars colliding 130 million light years ago, a kilonova.

More than that, how do I put all of this experience together? I certainly couldn't tell anyone without appearing crazy, and I don't know that I want to tell anyone anyway. How does one conceptualize this kind of outcome to life if it truly is the outcome of life? What more can I say or do? Maybe this is the 'Bridge of the Separator'? I hope it's not a bridge to purgatory.

And poor Guinness, what is he thinking about my being gone? I miss the little guy so much."

•

Madison has not sailed through life without making a few mistakes. She has had her share of them, certainly.

When just a little girl in grade school, she became quite bossy thinking she was smarter than other kids. That didn't last long when classmates teamed up against her and put her in her place as only grade school kids can. In high school her desire to be a perfectionist drove a lot of friends, mostly cliquish girls, away. She survived that by involving everyone she could in school governance and the school clubs of which she was a part. She also became less critical. It was a tough lesson to learn, as some friends never came back.

In college when convinced she had all the answers in religion, Madison found herself moved out of the mainstream of governance of the non-denominational church. That hurt her. She also found her reputation carried over to other associations, sororities and the dating scene. She recovered from those as well but not without some pain and disappointment, and she managed to get rid of the name "Know it all" which had been thrown at her by boys and girls alike.

Then she really fell in love for the first time - the very first time. It was heads-over-heels stuff. Madison met Dan in the college library, where else? Mutual attraction was instantaneous while everything she had read about true love, love at first sight, pheromones and total involvement was evident. Madison began meeting Dan in the library, and soon she and Dan scheduled classes together, meals together and free time together. Their romance, her first, was a passionate one. Madison was on a mission, and she fully committed herself to Dan.

Madison had read that one's heart actually plays a role coordinating emotional memory. The heart's electromagnetic field transmits signals through an energetic communication system operating just below a person's conscious level of awareness. "Hold on, Madison was thinking. Who knew? Yes my grandmother knew of course. She was the wise one."

•

Almost too familiar with the universe at this juncture in her adventure having seen it all, she knew the galactic center of the Milky Way is 24-28.4 kilo light years from earth in the direction of Sagittarius and Scorpio, and the Milky Way is over 100,000 light years across. She knew the European Space Agency (ESA) was measuring and mapping the Milky Way through 2020 and was studying makeup, position, motion and characteristics of a billion stars. It is estimated there are over 300 billion stars in the Milky Way and possibly 1 trillion in our sister galaxy, Andromeda. Madison even witnessed a supernova, the collapse of a super star.

"A light year is 5.9 trillion miles at 186,282 miles per second, she thought.
a kilo light year is 1,000 light years,
a mega light year is 1,000,000 light years, and
a giga light year is 1,000,000,000 light years."

•

"Have I stopped moving?" Madison couldn't tell. There was no noise, no feeling of movement, not a sensation of any kind. "What is happening now?" she wanted to ask. Madison was suspended - suspended in time, in space, in whatever this thing was that was carrying her to that light which still was barely visible. "Please tell me this isn't the end," she ventured to think even though the answer might have taken her over the edge. "Am I over the edge?" Madison almost laughed, if she could have laughed at all. "If I'm not over the edge by now, I never will be.

Really, I feel as if I am on a New York City subway that has stopped and the lights have gone out. Why is it so dark? Am I passing through something? Am I in something? Is it a black hole? A flash of panic went through Madison. "If I'm in a black hole, I'll never get out! Is this what I'm experiencing? Why would I be in a black hole?"

As if coming out of a tunnel, Madison again could see the universe. She could see multiple universes. She could visualize the Hawking superstring theory of multiple universes on vibrating strands of energy as well as the Rovelli quantum loop gravity theory of multiple universes, some beginning and some ending. "This truly is beginning to be too much for me to digest." Madison tried to gulp.

•

Madison's relationship with Dan didn't last. Dan wasn't ready for anything long-term or as intense at his age, especially since Madison was so much work and too into him.

She was crushed, so crushed that she swore off God and her idealistic view of love. "God you are not fair, and I hate you!" An emotional Madison had to vent. "Is my expectation of life all wrong? Is my understanding of God all wrong? Yes, God, you gave us free will - but to harm others? Why design project humanity just to let it fail like this. You have let so many people be hurt, to die and suffer needlessly for what? You have let nations destroy nations; you have let evil - yes, evil - exist. Why? What did I do to deserve this?" She was flush with emotions.

Madison decided to explore church denominations other than her own. She felt Buddhism talked to her and was fun, really fun and new although she found there were too many steps required to reach the ultimate goal - steps she wasn't about to fulfill.

"Hinduism, the Upanishads, Brahma - all too much, too many gods, too amorphous a religion for me. Judaism and Islam really have the same god and history up to certain points. Who knows? What I do know is that it isn't working for me right now thanks to Mister Dan. Ugh!"

Guinness was one of her only comforts. "This little guy is so loyal; he loves me regardless. Too bad men don't take a hint from dogs. Too bad men just don't 'get it'. I can't imagine ever falling in love again."

●

Madison came out of her 'tunnel' experience looking at Planet K2-18b, a super earth that orbits a sun-like star and is in the Leo Constellation. It is only 111 light years from earth. "That is 625 quadrillion miles from home." she thought as she zoomed by the mostly rock planet that has a gassy atmosphere just like earth. "Is there life on the planet? Why not?" It was getting easy to guess at this point in her journey.

•

Madison found herself dreaming about people, entities, places, far-out subjects she once imagined only drugs like LSD could awaken in her. She felt her body floating, arms spread and eyes closed floating through a likeness to water or air. She is warm, comfortably warm like having a blanket on her lap on a cool evening sitting in an old, horse drawn sleigh.

"Wait a minute!" Madison wanted to say. "Where are all these thoughts coming from? I have never floated on air, and I certainly have never been in a horse-drawn sleigh. And what's this about LSD? Other than reading about the decade of radicalism as some called it, the '60s, and the use of LSD, I've never seen it even with my brother's problems."

Madison had to gather her thoughts again. And thoughts were all she had. She knew she was conscious, but that was all. She wanted to end this trip now, as if she had the ability to do so.

"I have seen earth's moon, the fifth largest moon in our solar system. I have seen another black hole, a second in our solar system 100,000 times more massive than our sun. I have seen FRB 121102 - fast radio bursts originating 3 billion light years away from earth. I also have seen dinosaurs roaming earth 200 million years ago when I had traveled only 65 million light years from earth on this adventure. Try and figure that one out my friends where ever you are, since most of us struggled with trigonometry in the beginning." Madison knows light takes time to travel and looking at anything is tantamount to looking back in time. The further away something is in space the further back in time one sees.

"Oh well." a more than compromised Madison thought. "Maybe this is what the Tibetan Buddhists call Bardo? What do I know at this point?"

•

Madison enjoyed quoting the *Bible* mostly to herself. She became very aware of how boring it is for some to hear biblical verses, even Shakespeare and, yes, all that she was learning about cosmology. She did not want to become like an old or sick person who always talked about one thing, in their case, illnesses. Madison had to hold back and not talk about herself so much.

One verse struck home for her, however. *Romans* 5: Suffering produces endurance; endurance produces character; and character produces hope. Madison loved that verse more so now that she and Dan were history, and her future looked bleak. "Yesterday, today, soon tomorrow, the future...I'm a part of it already, and I don't know how it happened or that I like the fact it did happened."

"I suppose it is karma or something like that, what has happened to me. No, it can't be karma. What did I do to cause anything resulting in our breaking up? Of course, life could be over as I know it, now without Dan I have nothing to keep me going. Have I stepped into a hole and can't get out? Is this depression? God, help me please! Yes, God, I keep coming back to you and don't know why. Where do I go from here? I have never experienced pain like this, and I thought pain was only physical."

For Madison, stress was not always felt, yet it wasn't just out there someplace. Moreover there seemed to be no quick fix. Pain can be caused by the brain ordering reduced blood flow to an area of the body which resulting in pain and other symptoms of a greater problem. Reduced blood flow becomes oxygen deprivation. Getting over Dan is vitally important for Madison. She knows she is too young to be falling apart physically due to a broken romance. She has to do something about it, and that means getting over it now.

•

Madison had read about Bardo, of course. Bardo refers to the state of existence intermediate between two lives on earth. According to Tibetan tradition, after death and before one's rebirth when one's consciousness is not connected with a physical body, a person experiences a variety of phenomena. Once awareness is free from one's body, it creates its own reality such as in a dream. Dreams can be wonderful or frightening.

Having read parts of *The Tibetan Book of the Dead,* she knew the scripture of the old tradition of Tibetan Buddhism. The work's primary concern is the nature of the mind and its projection which exist in the external world. The projections appear immediately after death.

She knew the book referred to the interval of suspension after death, visions without any nature of their own not like illusions. "The whole of space shines like a blue light, while a white light shines representing the purified element of water."

She also skimmed *The Tripitaka*, the word of Buddha, the *Mahayana Sutras* and *The Tibetan Book of the Dead*, the major books of Buddhism.

"Buddhists do not believe in a human soul. What and where does that leave me now on this adventure?"

•

Madison felt she had been inside this thing forever but knew it had been no time at all, not even a second. Her thoughts were all-at-once together again, seemingly not measured by a factor called time. The pinpoint of light still was there, and so were the surreal images surrounding her like a scene from a sci-fi movie.

Madison found herself viewing her mother and father's funerals. She saw her sister's grandchildren and their children. Images of fantastic robotics, computers and technology unlike anything experienced by her a second ago were not only advanced but some out-of-date already. Again she asked herself, "How can that be?" There were new leaders of countries, phenomenal advancements in medicine, changes in styles as well as food preferences, the climate and people's attitudes.

"I'm beginning to understand." Madison suddenly thought. "Why was I so slow in putting this adventure together? I don't need to cry; I don't need to worry; I don't need to anticipate, all of which I can't do anyway while I'm here. It's all OK. Everything in life as I know it and more is with me, and it is OK."

•

Madison was in New York City for an educational meeting regarding new math for middle school students. She played a role in the meeting functioning as an experienced teacher looking for new methods to teach. Early in her teaching career Madison quickly became aware of students who simply could not grasp mathematics as a result of their upbringing and background, and she wanted to find answers.

"Kids are wired differently than us, and don't we know it!" she spoke. "Just look at their habits today. They sit on their iPhones, X Boxes and laptops - most of laptops having been given to them by their schools. We know their brains are growing rapidly at their age, and we know we have to make changes to our curriculum to adapt. This information isn't new for any of you, but the fact that we are falling behind in making math more challenging may be new and even unacceptable. Take our lead from the software industry, they change and adapt all the time. The question with which I struggle day to day is that of engagement. Are we engaging students or entertaining them?"

While staying at the new Marriott immediately off Times Square, Madison took a walk with girlfriends and happened to come upon a gathering of practicing

Buddhists welcoming the Dalai Lama to the city. Security was tight, but Madison didn't look or act threatening and passed through the crowd of followers unusually easy. Call it timing, happenstance or karma, Madison came face to face with the Dalai Lama who took her hand, thanked her for coming and asked that she continue to focus on working with and aiding humanity worldwide. The Dalai Lama's bodyguards were shocked and embarrassed that they missed Madison coming through the mass of humanity and trying to get glimpse of the celebrity.

Madison couldn't speak. The Dalai Lama held her hand and smiled while acknowledging Madison's stunned reaction to seeing him so very close. He looked at her with a power in his eyes that continued to overwhelm her and suggested the two had met before and will meet again. Absolutely lost at this point, Madison smiled and agreed. She had no idea what he meant by that comment, as she never considered it a possibility.

Later in her hotel room Madison flopped on the bed with her head on the pillow thinking "We have met before? We will meet again? Looks like I had better get back into studying Buddhism if I am going to meet him again. But...What are the chances? What were the chances of today happening?"

Madison's life had changed again. This time it wasn't all about Madison. "Are coincidences one way of God's communicating with us?" she thought.

•

Madison being a good Catholic, loved Thomas Aquinas, 1225-1274. In his work, *Summa Theologica*, he wrote: "It is clear that inanimate bodies reach their end not by chance but by intention. There is, therefore, an intelligent personal being by who[m] everything in nature is ordered to its end.

The order of the universe only can be the result of a conscious intelligence, and the existence of something and its essence are separate."

Aquinas' five ways to prove the existence of God influenced the rise of scholasticism and provided framework for the Roman Catholic Church, and Madison was conversant in all five.

1. Argument from motion – There has to be an unmoved mover.

2. Argument from cause – There has to be an uncaused cause capable of imparting existence to all other things.
3. Argument from necessity – We cannot conceive of a time when nothing existed.

4. Argument from degree – The gradation of beings: dogs, man, angels, God are visible proof.
5. Argument from design – A design (order of the universe) can only be the design of a conscious intelligence.

•

"The question," thought Madison "is how quantum mechanics, wave mechanics, gravity, space and time fit with Aquinas?" The basic postulate is that a particle (wave) can be present anywhere, and an event can happen in several, sometimes countless ways.

If quantum physics introduces the unpredictability and randomness of its science, then particles can exist in more than one place at a time. "Swell!" thought Madison. "How do I explain that?"

Quantum entanglement results in particle interacting and becoming linked so that an action performed on one instantly influences the other, even if they are far apart. "Is there is a quantum code for everything. This must be the key." Madison was determined to understand this even though she was way over her head regarding science. "Three fermions make a quark. I keep coming back to that theory. Maybe that really is the location of my consciousness?"

"Without quantum mechanics there would be no transistors, but they remain mysterious. They do not describe what happens to a physical system but only how a physical system affects another physical system." Carlo Rovelli, *Seven Brief Lessons on Physics*

•

"Mother, Mother!" Madison tried to scream. "I understand now. All of us thought you were no longer lucid when you kept remembering things only your cardiologist or heart donor could have known. What is that all about? We kept saying.

 I understand now; I understand so very clearly now."

Madison's mother received a heart transplant a few years ago. After the surgery, Madison's mother began remembering events in the life of the donor. The thoughts were vivid and proven true after consultations with doctors and family of the donor. On occasion Madison's mother even spoke with the accent of the donor. Madison began studying energetic cardiology, cellular memory, the electromagnetic pattern generated by the heart, electromagnetic fields, and quantum fields of the global bio energy field inside the body. All of it was beyond her limited scientific background but so very interesting.

"Now and only now does it all make sense. I'm living it with you, Mother," she thought. "Whatever memory consists of, wherever memory is kept, however memory works, it is everywhere now. Maybe it's all about the fermions, bosons, quarks and quantum bits, qubits, about which I have been reading. Maybe that's where memory is stored?"

•

Madison began to study Buddhism with a renewed interest still knowing she knew she would never be able to practice the religion as required. She fully understood the Dalai Lama's comments but struggled to understand why he made them to her at such an accidental meeting in of all places, New York City.

"Maybe I'm doomed? My friends shunned me until I came off my high horse, and then Dan dumped me. Now I meet a man who overwhelms me with a depth of understanding I'll never have. So, how do I teach kids to better understand something like math when I can't even understand life?" Madison rambled on and on with her friends.

When she found the 13th Century Italian theologian that began to put it together for her, everything changed. His comment about "an intelligent personal being by whom everything in nature is ordered to its end" finally brought her head out of the clouds. Thomas Aquinas' understanding of the universe made sense to

Madison. More than that, it gave her hope. Aquinas' five ways to prove the existence of God became her mantra whenever positioning her direction in life

compared to others trying to find theirs. She did that carefully, however, knowing how overbearing she could be - a lesson learned from school days.

Equally important to Madison was her new understanding of the universe. "Aquinas had it right when it came to the order of the universe being the result of a conscious intelligence." Madison would go on. "But, where is the answer about the extent of the universe? How can the universe continue to expand? Where is it going? Will we ever find out? Maybe Hawking and Rovelli have it right regarding multiple universes? How will we ever find out? Will I find out now?"

In college, Madison read a book by Ian Barbour, 1923-2013, Physicist & Theologian, *Issues in Science and Religion*. A former Carleton College professor who retired before Madison entered college in his home town of Northfield, wrote "God's action in the world can be thought of as the communication of information from DNA to computer networks."

Ian Barbour also wrote "The Big Bang Theory fits with traditional Christian ideas. This is the universe we might expect if we have a personal God interested in conscious human beings. Death is a necessary aspect of an evolutionary world. One generation has to die for another generation to come into being."

Madison also read Stephen Hawking who wrote "DNA itself points to intelligence.

•

Later in her studies Madison came across the following. Heart transplant recipients frequently report having memories, speech patterns and behaviors associated with the donor of the transplanted heart. Pearsall 1998; Schwartz 1999

Energetic cardiology offers a new system theoretical approach that may be helpful to explain the capacity of all cells to store information. Russek and Schwartz 1994, 1996

The electromagnetic pattern generated by the heart as the largest electromagnetic signal generator in the body also travels into space and continues indefinitely. Rein 1998

A little girl who received a heart donated by another girl who had been murdered was able to identify the killer of the donor and assisted police in having the killer convicted. Karl H. Maret, M.D., M. Eng. / ExplorePub.com

It is a truism of classical physics that information contained in energy, once produced, does not vanish spontaneously. Orear 1962, Energetic Cardiology, Cellular Memory. Madison was speechless when learning all of this.

•

"I see it! My God, I really see it! Time to hold on, Madison!" she wanted to say. "I see the beginning; I see the end; I see everything in between.

It's beautiful! It's wonderful! Yes, it is incomprehensible, indescribable, inconceivable, and unutterable as Buddha said when discussing death of the body and the rebirth of the ego.

God, or whoever you are, whatever you are, I am so sorry I didn't understand before. But could I have understood before?"

Madison saw the earliest universe 13.7 billion years ago immediately after the quantum fluctuation. She saw gravity and light with the onset of cosmic expansion. She saw Omega Centauri forming as a global cluster in the earliest of the Milky Way 11.5 billion years ago. Andromeda began forming in front of her eyes 10 billion years ago. Then she saw the Milky Way actually forming as a result of the presence of dark matter and dark energy 8.8 billion years ago. Alpha Centauri began forming 6.5 billion years ago. Then with the cosmic expansion, Madison saw the beginning of earth 4.54 billion years ago along with the solar system. She witnessed the formation of organic compounds and earliest life 4.3 billion years ago. She witnessed the beginning of photosynthesis, the development of oxygen, the first sexual reproduction and finally human development. She saw it all including planet Gliese 832c with five times the mass of earth and a similar temperature which might make it inhabitable. Gliese is 16 light years from earth, Madison learned only recently. But now, amazingly, she has seen it.

•

Madison, the analytical mathematician through and through, began coming to some very interesting conclusions about life and the world in which we live.

First, she accepted the possibility that God is teaching us how he thinks not just with mathematics but also with writing code, software and the use of the computer. "It has to be." Madison suggested. "If our knowledge truly is constrained to mathematics and the science of the natural world, we can't go further without help. Does God come into play here? If the universe has a purpose, then the creator surely will let us know at some point."

Second she thought, "If we live in a four dimensional world i.e. length, width, depth and time, maybe God will allow us to enter a fifth or sixth dimension at some point? Even near death experiences may be another way that God is allowing us to gather information about how we get to where we are going when we die? If not, then why are so many - if not all - of the near death experiences worldwide so much alike?

I do know one thing for sure. Religion continues to search for God - the lawmaker; science, the originator - energy. No one will find either until God allows it."

•

Madison saw the moon traveling around the earth at 2,288 mph while maintaining a counter-clockwise orbit like that of earth. With the earth rotating at 1000 mph, the moon orbits earth every 27.322 days.

She saw the moon also rotating on its axis every 27 days which makes it appear still, not moving. Synchronous rotation is similar for a majority of moons in the entire solar system. The moon's orbit is elliptical while the same side, the near side, always faces the earth.

Meanwhile she also realized earth's moon is larger than Pluto.

Then she saw a mid-sized black hole that has been found near the center of the Milky Way in a cloud of molecular gas. It was discovered by finding massive gravitational forces moving around the center of the cloud which could have been formed after the former core of a dwarf galaxy was absorbed by the Milky Way. It is the second black hole discovered in the galaxy.

Surprisingly she witnessed fifteen bright light radio pulses from a dwarf galaxy 3 billion light years away that are being studied. The fast radio bursts (FRBs) are super fast, very powerful radio signals. The cause of FRB 121102 signals is not known, and Madison, not surprisingly, did not have answer.

•

"Oh my God!" shouted Madison. "I think I feel the presence of ... of maybe God, the creator, the sustainer, the deliverer, the source of everything? Or do I feel pure energy?"

Madison fought to understand all of this and shouted "Oh my God!" when she thought she was about to give up. But she had nothing to give up, plus she didn't have the option to give up. All she was doing was heading toward a light, a pinpoint at the end of the tunnel in which she was moving. She had just seen more than anyone on earth ever had seen, and she felt even more - intense fear, intense love, intense hate and anger all at once - but she couldn't comprehend it all. Yet she knew now, for sure, a presence with her, in her, around her was taking her on this ride, this adventure into the past, present and future.

"Who else or what else could I feel other than God?" Madison had learned enough about heaven and hell when a kid. She professed to believe in God as well as the devil and all his works and all his ways. She accepted the Judeo-Christian tradition of a Savior, and she accepted the person who came as a Savior. But not until now did she understand what it all meant. She asked "Is my conception of life and death all wrong? Is my conception of God all wrong?"

Madison had dabbled in Buddhism with her friends. She understood the four noble truths of Buddhism, the focus on spiritual enlightenment and even Buddhism's lack of a need for a god. "Even Buddha never attained Nirvana." she thought. "Am I? Am I, by chance, now attaining Nirvana?"

She even read more about Hinduism and other parts of the Upanishads while coming to understand the highest purpose of the Vedas, the concept of Braham, ultimate reality and Atman, one's soul entering another form. "I don't know who wrote this stuff, really, but doesn't it make sense to me now? Yes, doesn't it make sense to me right now? Does the divine live in all beings? Namaste, she thought. I bow to the divine in you, whoever, whatever, wherever you are."

•

"Midwestern girl travels to another universe and returns home having seen, heard and touched it all - including God!" Madison could see the headlines in the Minneapolis Star Tribune and in her hometown's local newspaper, and she could hear the reporters on WCCO Radio and TV.

"What headlines?" she gasped. "What is wrong with me? Who do I think I am? Not only that, but I haven't touched God or anything like that. All I have done is to reach the light which is...I don't know. I don't know yet.

But I am here, someplace in space-time I guess, having travelled a great distance in a picosecond or faster. How much time is that for people, loved ones or Guinness on earth, years, decades, centuries? I don't know and don't dare guess, not knowing how I would handle the truth."

•

Madison has come to believe everything she is experiencing is that which all of the theologians, philosophers and scientists have been describing. "Buddhists call it Atman; Christianity, Heaven. Teilhard de Chardin calls it the Omega Point; Julien Huxley, Transhumanism. Moses led people to the Promised Land; Plato, a pure and powerful light. McMillan says Lawmaker; scientists, energy - the source of energy. Zoroaster had his House of Song; Socrates, Heavenly Meadows. Judaism calls it salvation; Islam, the Day of Judgment. Even Brian McLaren called it the 'Unimaginable light of God's presence.' They all are saying the same thing using different words.

And how did I get here? Fermions and bosons, waves/wavelets which hold my consciousness, my memory, my being, my soul while traveling at a speed I can't comprehend? Oh yes, three fermions make a quark, and the quark could be the key to holding my consciousness. Do I need to remember that anymore?

I believe I am at the door of the Lawmaker, the source of energy itself."

Madison was approaching the light, the pinpoint of light which seemed so very, very far away only a fraction of a second ago. "Or was it a picosecond ago?" she thought. Madison was becoming more aware of her present environment. The light was there in front of her. It was radiant, powerful, unimaginable, transcendent, bright, and warm and healing. She thought "Is it Heaven; is it Nirvana; is it Hell; is it Purgatory; is it the Day-of-Judgment? Is it good? Oh yes, it is good! It has to be good. I know now."

Madison knew she had died; it was certain. She knew she had left her physical body behind and now knew she was consciousness alone. She knew she was essence, being, soul, spirit only. She could think; she could reason; she could rationalize. She knew she was created to become this, the image of the entity that created her. The image was that of pure energy. She understood quantum mechanics; she understood gravitation; she understood thermodynamics; she understood weak and strong nuclear force. She understood relativity.

Madison has taken the last great adventure and had arrived. She had arrived at the light.

•

Madison's was in her mid twenties when she was hit by the oncoming car. Having studied Morris Massey in college sociology courses, she knew her identity and personality had formed. Madison was a mature woman. She knew kids up to the age of seven were like sponges absorbing everything around them while accepting most of it as true. She knew the kids she taught, ages eight through twelve were apt to copy people they liked especially parents, and kids fourteen through twenty one copied their peers. This was her business, knowing her students and how they learned.

Imagining her reaction to the reality of living through this kind of learning experience was a different story. Of course she would like to think that she could, but in reality the journey would be too much for her. Or would it?

Madison had arrived at this point in life knowing what she liked to do, and that was to teach. She knew what she wanted in a relationship, someone intelligent with a sense of humor and style. She knew her lifestyle was a simple one that included the likes of yet another Guinness, a beagle she rescued when he was a pup. She considered herself non-judgmental and accepting. She also knew she had flaws just like everyone else. Madison was ready to take on life when the accident arrested everything – but her consciousness.

Madison now agreed with and understood Sir Julien Sorell Huxley, 1887-1975, Evolutionary Biologist and the brother of Aldous. He wrote "I believe in Transhumanism. Once there are enough people who can truly say that, the human species will be on the threshold of a new kind of existence, as different from ours as ours is from that of Peking man. It will at last consciously be fulfilling its real destiny. Humankind as evolution becomes conscious of itself."

Madison also understood Carlo Rovelli's theory his book, *Seven Brief Lessons on Physics*, when he writes that he believes our species will not last long. "We belong to a short-lived genus of species. All of our cousins are already extinct."

And she agreed with Stephen Hawking's call for colonization of another planet within 100 earth years [2117] due to climate change, nuclear war, overdue asteroid strikes, engineered viruses and population growth.

•

Regarding matter, which has mass and increases in proportion to its speed, Madison knew matter cannot go faster than the speed of light. An object would appear to lengthen if observed approaching the speed of light. It would appear to compress to someone on board an object approaching the speed of light. Only quanta, the same as photons which are bundles of electromagnetic energy and have no intrinsic mass, no rest mass, can move at the speed of light. Madison was no longer matter.

Madison knew her consciousness - waves or wavelets - moved at the speed of light or much, much faster. She also knew everything in the universe was either energy or matter. Most important, she knew she was energy, pure energy.

PART TWO

The Return

THE LAST GREAT ADVENTURE

Part Two
The Return

    The light above Madison was blinding. It also was out of focus. There seemed to be a buzz of activity around her, while the smell of antiseptic was pungent and unusually hard on her nasal passages. "Now what do I do?" She thought.

    Her hand was being held by an experienced M.D. who studied her eyes and talked softly. "Madison? Madison? Are you awake? I'm very close to recommending another spinal tap if you still can't answer. You have not been responding for too long."

    "Spinal tap!" Madison awoke and reacted to those words with a sharp retort. "No, please! No spinal tap for me, honest. I am aware of everything, and I am ready to leave wherever I am. Let me get up and walk a bit. That'll clear my head, I know."

    "Madison, hold on. Your body still is bruised, and you sustained quite a blow to your head. More than a few days of bed rest is in order, and leaving the hospital is not an option right now." Dr. Pike talked while holding Madison's hand firmly, preventing her from trying to get out of bed. "Look at it this way, Madison, we have an excellent food service here, cable TV is yours to use, and already you have friends anxious to see you. Plus the wonderful smell of those flowers should make you more relaxed. You have no idea how lucky you are to be alive after the head-on crash."

    "What crash? What is today? Where am I? You are a very nice person, Doctor, but I don't even know who you are." Madison wasn't able to think clearly. She was experiencing amnesia but continued to attempt to prove she was in control of the situation. "Let me see now, I'll get dressed, call a cab and head home."

    "You know, Madison, I'm beginning to think the concussion may have been more severe than the MRI indicated, and I'm going to recommend a higher dosage of anticoagulants and blood thinners just to be sure you come out of your heavy fog without any after effects." Dr. Pike was in the tenth year of her emergency room duties as a psychiatrist and had seen a number of head injuries. This one bothered her, however, especially with the lengthy conversations Madison was having with herself. Dr. Pike knew her patient was not a scientist, and she was amazed by the level of information Madison reported about the universe, relativity and quantum mechanics while she was unconscious. The key factor for the doctor was that of Madison's unconscious expertise. "What am I looking at here? Is this a near death experience or something more dramatic than I've never seen?"

●

Madison sat in bed restless for what seemed days, while everyone she knew wanted to visit her but fully understood why only her mother, Sandra Lee, was allowed. Meanwhile Sandra Lee came to Madison's hospital as soon as she learned of the accident. Outspoken and having become most demanding, she took charge insisting that, Roy, her husband stay at home with Guinness. "She will be fine once she gets some rest. There simply isn't any need for you to drive to Minneapolis, rent a hotel room and spend so much money now that Dr. Pike has told us Madison will be OK with a little bed rest. Plus you know how you are in the hospital - restless, bored, and hungry. Stay home and take care of Guinness. Madison would never forgive you if something happened to him or if you put him into a kennel." Sandra Lee always took the overprotective mother's approach to all that had happened in the family ever since the difficult and challenging times she had with her oldest son. Her husband nodded in agreement simply to avoid an argument, in that everyone was feeling so much stress after Madison's accident.

"The last thing that woman needs is more of that miserable, hormone cortisol in her system," so thought Sandra Lee's husband. Plus she can stay at her overly controlling sister's home again, which isn't my choice - ever."

●

Madison tried to sit up in bed while being so very eager to talk about her experience. She had an understanding of life, death, theology, philosophy and science that surpassed anything about which she had read. In actuality it surpassed all that only a handful of people would know. "I have so much to say - but to whom, and how in the world do I tell this story? Who would believe me? I can start with a priest since I don't know any philosophers, and then I can visit with a physicist at my former college. If I can teach kids to understand mathematical formulas with ease, surely I can talk the language of theology and science with both a priest and a physicist and explain all that I have seen." Madison had developed a rather serious habit of talking to herself and continued to do so.

Moreover, Madison felt her arms, legs, head and stomach with her hands. "I have them; they are here; I can see them as well. Something isn't right though, and I can't pinpoint it yet. I feel different physically, and I'm sensing Dr. Pike recognizes that. If I had a near death experience, would I wind up younger or older? If that is what I really experienced, wouldn't I be the same when it was over? Who knows? Grandfather would say 'Only the Shadow knows', and he might be right. Whatever, whomever I encountered when I reached the light knows too, that's for sure. But the light, where is the light now?"

•

"Doctor Pike, I heard someone say that I was dead. Is that possible?"

"More than possible Madison, your heart stopped, and blood to your brain was cut off. However, certain parts of one's brain including yours remain active after death, and you may well have heard the ER doctor pronounce you dead. In reality, you may have heard lots of conversations after having been pronounced dead."

"Pronounced me dead? You have to be kidding me. I am alive aren't I? Everything I do tells me I am alive."

"You are alive all right, and the trauma you experienced is alive and well in your mind."

"Doctor, you have no idea what is alive and well in my brain. It's too much to handle."

"I have a feeling I do, Madison. Do you want to talk about it?"

"Talk about it? I don't know that I dare, and I don't know that anyone will believe me. Just how open minded are you, Dr. Pike?"

"Madison, I have a PhD in Psychiatry, and I'm also a practicing physician. Mine might be a perfect background for all you have to say. It could be your lucky day to have me as your doctor."

"Doctor, do you believe I was dead?"

"Clinically dead, yes you were. But..."

"So what did I experience? It was real, I know it was."

"Madison, let's slow down for a minute. I have witnessed more than a few death pronouncements after which the patient came to life again having had experiences unlike anything we deemed possible in the time frame she was thought dead. Some refer to the happenings as near death experiences. Possibly you have had a near death experience, but yours was different, very different. You told me everything you witnessed, everything you experienced while still unconscious."

"How did I do that?"

"I'm not sure yet, so let's start at the beginning. You were involved in an automobile accident that left you clinically dead. Your heart wasn't beating, and you had no blood flow to your brain – none! Now here is the difference between your experience and others. We bagged you and sent you to the morgue. Yes, that sounds crass, but that's what we do when a person dies in the hospital. Once it had been confirmed that you were dead, we quickly prepared your body for the morgue. Since we couldn't find anyone who had responsibility for you, it took a day to find and contact your parents. That's when all hell broke loose, pardon my language.

The personnel at the funeral home found you alive in the morgue, and they nearly went ballistic. It had never happened to them before or any other funeral home that we know. You were rushed back to the hospital immediately with a body temp of 42 degrees. How you survived will be a topic for the research folks. All I know is that you did survive.

Thing is, your brain seemed to be functioning even as we began treating you again, and we are not sure that it ever shut down. That's when I came into the picture and began listening to you describe your experience or better yet experiences, as there were many. Actually, I sensed you somehow were thinking about your experiences, but it sounded like you were talking with me."

"That can't be. I was alone all the time. Even when I approached the light, I was alone."

"Yes, the light. That's a good place to start, Madison, so tell me about the light."

"I can't. I reached it, but then I found myself listening to you. And now I am spooked. How could all of that have happened only to find myself in a hospital talking with a stranger? I'm sorry. I don't know how else to refer to you in this context."

"That's perfectly OK. We won't be strangers for long, of that I can assure you."

Just then Sandra Lee came through the door crying and moving towards Madison. Dr. Pike backed away while Madison didn't say a word until her mother hugged her, covered her with tears, another blanket and sat holding her hand.

Extending her hand, Dr. Pike spoke. "I am Dr. Pike; we talked on the phone. Your daughter appears to be doing very, very well. Did the nurses brief you before you came into the room?"

"Oh yes, yes they did, and I'm so glad you are here, Dr. Pike. Is she going to be OK?"

"There is no reason to think otherwise. Other than a few minor scratches and bruises, Madison is fine. Our main concern now is her memory."

"That accident, that driver, does anyone know why he crossed the median? Hitting my sweet little girl, what a terrible thing that is."

"The driver of the other automobile is dead, Sandra, and as you know, he was catapulted through the windshield in his car and landed on the street. Why he crossed the median, we don't know yet and possibly never will."

"Oh, I'm so sorry. Life can be so dangerous at times in the city and even in our small town of Cottonwood, but I am so relieved Madison now is OK and has you as her doctor. You were so very nice on the phone."

"Thank you. However, I was just about to put Madison through some mental exercises to check on her progress. My guess is that it will take no more than twenty five minutes. Would you mind stepping out, maybe have a cup of coffee so that there are no distractions?"

"Surely, however I wouldn't be a problem. Isn't that right, Madison?"

"Sandra, I believe you, and knowing that you are here is a plus for Madison. But these exercises are designed to have the patient totally alone with a doctor - no chance for even an outside sniffle or cough. We are entering a new stage of recovery for the patient."

"Coffee it is then, doctor. Twenty five minutes OK?"

"Absolutely, and thank you."

•

Sandra Lee left, and Madison immediately returned her attention to Dr. Pike. "Nice job handling my mother. I'll start where I think I became aware that something was happening. I felt like I was suspended in air or something like that. I was having visions, illusions without any real substance of their own. You know, they seemed real but not tangible. The whole of space shined with an almost bluish light along with that white light at the end. The bluish color looked like pure water."

"Madison, when did the feeling of being suspended occur?"

"Immediately when I saw the car come across the median and hit me head on. I also heard someone pronounce me dead while others stopped talking and seemed busy cleaning the room. No, no, that was later. I went from driving the car to floating out there somewhere. I know it. The light was..."

"Madison, don't move so quickly through this. You know Buddhists believe you create your own reality once your awareness is freed from your body. That reality could be a wonderful dream or a horrible nightmare. Once you are dead, consciousness can experience a variety of phenomena - according to Buddhism. If you died, Madison, everything you feel happened may well have happened including the blue space and white light."

"Died? Do you really think I died, and if so how did I come back? If I really did experience all that phenomena, why did I come back?"

"Good question that I can't answer, and no one can for that matter. That's why I want to stay with the conversation about your experience after being hit by the car. Obviously something happened since you were found alive at the mortuary when you should have been dead. Not only that, but you survived death in one piece, whole mentally and physically. I want to find out why?"

"Doctor Pike, I was alive all the time, conscious, aware. I was able to think my way through whatever I was going through. It was as if I existed in between two entities, life and something else."

"Madison, you are talking as if you have more than a cursory understanding of Buddhism, Tibetan Buddhism to be exact. The state in which you found yourself is called Bardo in *The Tibetan Book of the Dead*. Do you think your studies in Buddhism led you to imagine that?"

"I wish it were that easy. I really don't know, although I never gave much thought to Bardo, now that you remind me of the term. But I do feel that the experience was real, very real."

"Did you smell anything, feel anything, or hear anything?"

"No, I don't think so, although I thought about it when moving toward the light. It took me a while to recognize I was thinking, much less recognize I was going somewhere. And Doctor, it happened so very fast, faster than anything you or I can imagine."

"One more question before Sandra Lee returns. Are you familiar with out of body experiences?"

"No, not really. I have read about them and even questioned myself while going wherever I was going. Out of body seems too unreal, impossible, really weird."

"Here comes your mom. However, there is nothing weird about you or strange. We'll talk again later."

•

Later meant after Sandra Lee left for her sister's house and the hospital was quieting down from the day's activities. Dr. Pike often slept at the hospital in staff quarters, so meeting with Madison later was very convenient. "This is going to be a real challenge." Dr. Pike was thinking out loud. "Whatever I can learn from this event will be invaluable to science and religion if either is willing to accept the impossible. And for Madison, I only hope she can deal with all she has gone through and what she is about to go through. Post traumatic stress syndrome surely will be in play here. Not only that but chronic traumatic encephalopathy, CTE, is a major concern, and no question more deep brain scanning is needed. I'll mention it to her hoping she will see the benefit of all our imaging capabilities."

"Hi. How are you feeling and was your mother at all comforting?"

"Dr. Pike, she has changed a lot since I left home, although I'll attribute the negative side of that comment to my brother who drove her to the wall. I'm sure age has a lot to do with her change as well. The kids are gone; she and dad are living as empty nesters; and she is not as sharp as she used to be."

"Welcome to the real world, Madison. My dad used to say 'To such a state we are all hastening.' It appears that both your mother and father don't want to face too much in the way of crisis in the future. Not certain how that will work out for them, but certainly let's hope for the best."

"Dr. Pike, I was in a wormhole, I know it. It was anti-gravitational, and it was borrowing energy from one region of space that didn't have energy at all. I was there; I was moving through the universe, universes, unlike anything science has confirmed before. How else can I describe it? I was floating, falling, twisting, turning, and rolling so fast I thought I was going to lose it. But I didn't. Why?"

"That's what I want to figure out, Madison. I am aware of near death experiences, but yours, if it was a near death experience, is very, very different. You saw so much and then repeated it to me when you were unconscious. It's that unconsciousness that puzzles me as much as your journey."

"Journey, it wasn't a journey, Dr. Pike. It was more of an adventure, one from which I returned in one piece. I remember what was said by John Steinbeck. 'People don't take trips; trips take people.' That's it! That's me. I was taken on a trip, again I'll say an adventure, and it has to be of some significance."

"I'm hoping so for your sake. You experienced so much trauma that surely you have a message to share, and I personally think that is why you returned, if indeed you returned from anywhere."

"Returned? Returned from where? I reached the light, but that was it. I have no recollection of the light other than it was wonderful, powerful, radiant."

"And healing, unimaginable and transcendent, you said to me when unconscious. Oh yes, I remember. I didn't record your conversation, but I surely wish that I had."

"You remember that? How...Why...Oh God, I'm lost even more now than before."

"No need to worry, Madison. If you survived your adventure, remembering most of it will be a piece of cake. Plus you have me here to help you through the process."

"I hope so. I surely hope so. But then there is my mother. How are you going to keep her out of the conversation?"

"Let me deal with that, Madison. This is not the first time I have had an overly protective and demanding mother with whom to deal. Plus she doesn't know me yet. Sandra Lee will calm down as you get better, and all she will notice is your physical improvement. Seems the physical improvement overrides the mental state with parents. Don't know why - well, I do - but the fact is I can manage her anxiety."

"Doctor, I saw the Big Bang. I saw the expansion, the inflation and the beginning of gravity in this universe composed of quantum particles, graviton waves. I am a witness to the theory that the universe has a finite age and that it has evolved over time through cooling - yes, cooling. How in the world does the universe cool? I ask that question but know the answer because the intense heat generated by the quantum fluctuation, the Big Bang, cooled. The universe cooled and expanded creating the foundation of structures through gravitational collapse. Doctor Pike, I saw all of this. That is Stephen Hawking's description as well. How in the world do I know it? It has to be since I've seen it."

"I can't testify to all that, Madison, but my limited understanding of cosmology tells me you are correct. Not only that, but it agrees with all that you told me when you were unconscious. That is a most important step for you. You remember."

"I even saw primordial black holes being produced directly from external pressure in the first moments after the Big Bang. Even "Hawking Radiation" was visible."

"Looks like you are getting tired. As your doctor, I would be remiss if I didn't suggest you get some sleep. Plus you have your mother coming in tomorrow morning early. Let's say good night, Madison."

"Thanks, Dr. Pike."

•

Madison slept rather soundly after talking with Dr. Pike. She fell asleep thinking about therapy and all that Dr. Pike offered her. Then she started dreaming about Ptolemy who she felt she had met and knew. That was about 150 CE with Ptolemy claiming the sun revolved around the earth. It made sense then. But along came Copernicus in 1534 CE, who Madison also felt she had met and knew, with his theory that the earth and other planets revolved around the sun. It made more sense then as well. Madison woke herself up quickly fearing something she had seen.

"Andromeda, our sister galaxy, is 2.5 million light years away, and it is on a path to collide with the Milky Way in 4.5 million years. I witnessed the collision! My God, I witnessed the collision. Dr. Pike, Dr. Pike we have to make certain people on earth know that."

"Madison, I am your evening nurse, John. Are you OK? You have been screaming for Dr. Pike who is not here."

"I'm OK. I'm OK. It's just that I know things the world needs to know."

"I believe you do. However, I suggest you write them down and wait until Dr. Pike comes in tomorrow. Writing your thoughts down also will give you more clarity especially in view of your head injury."

"John, do you know what is going on at CERN, The European Organization for Nuclear Research?"

"You are losing me, Madison. I am familiar with names like Andromeda and the Milky Way, of course, but CERN, if I am pronouncing it correctly, is out of my league."

"John, I saw what they accomplished. They found a particle smaller than a quark. They isolated a fermion, which some call the God particle."

"OK Madison. I suggest you put your head on the pillow and get some sleep. A fermion, huh? And four and a half million years isn't exactly tomorrow. You will be better engaged talking with Dr. Pike, for sure."

•

"Dr. Pike, I moved through space while witnessing a cosmological constant, dark energy - negative pressure - driving space apart creating more space and more dark energy. Energy was creating energy, pure energy from the source - the light towards which I was heading. And space, the universe, was expanding just like Hubble said. You know Edwin Hubble, of course. And, yes, it was expanding faster the further away from the center of the universe as if it were a balloon growing and growing. And Dr. Pike, I could see the end and all that is outside of the universe. I also moved outside the four dimensions of space into the fifth, a world of dreams. I saw it as a hologram, a curvature in the fabric of space time with three dimensions on a two dimensional surface. Think about it, Dr. Pike. I saw in total six dimensions of space including length, width, depth, and time - past, present and future. Yes, I lived in the past, the present and the future while on the adventure.

What do you think? Is it off to acute psychiatric services for me or do I still have my wits about me?"

"I'm listening, Madison, and I am not making any judgments concerning what I am hearing. No, by the way, after listening to you when you were unconscious, all I can do is be very accepting of what I hear now. Are you nuts? No. Absolutely not! What you have to share with me and the world may well change it though. That's a big order, but that is exactly the reality with which we are dealing. I am a psychiatrist, and I don't question your sanity at all. We'll have to wait and see what a theologian and physicist have to say."

"Dr. Pike, what I am saying is that I witnessed electrons with a negative charge collide with positrons with a positive charge and annihilate each other resulting in pure energy. Isn't that what science is looking for, pure energy? Isn't that what the book *Angels & Demons* was looking for, the God particle?"

"I don't know, Madison, but I certainly feel you do. But how and why are the real questions. We still have a long way to go with all of this, and I know you have much, much more to say."

"Just before all of this happened to me, I read of subatomic particles penetrating rock. The rock was an Egyptian pyramid in which they found additional tunnels and rooms never thought findable before. The subatomic particle was a muon - a wave or wavelet - that enabled cosmic ray imaging. Dr. Pike, I understand all of that now, and all I am is a Midwest, middle school math teacher. How in the world could I possibly understand all of that?"

"How about having a glass of milk and an Oreo cookie, Madison? We can understand that, for sure. Your mother will be here shortly, and I'd like to get you in a relaxed state of mind. Sandra Lee is going to raise your blood pressure a bit, and I'd like that blood pressure to start lower than it is right now."

•

Madison's mother walked into her room with a big surprise for her daughter. Sandra Lee was all smiles and acted as if she had found Jason's Golden Fleece. "Madison, look who I found wandering the floor looking for you, Dan."

It was Dan - Madison's first and only love in this "project humanity" as she preferred to call life. Dan, looking good and full of excitement and concern, walked towards Madison's hospital bed.

"Hi. I heard you took an automobile square on. Some of your college friends called me hoping you would perk up if I came to the hospital. I have been working in St. Paul since we graduated which makes getting to Fairview Southdale here in Edina no issue at all. How are they treating you?"

Madison looked at Dan and suddenly began to cry. It was the first time she cried since the accident. "How do you stop loving someone for whom you cared so much?" She thought. Her mind began spinning a bit, but her focus stayed with

Dan even though she couldn't pull all her thoughts together. Madison's emotions were spilling out.

"Dan, I remember you so very well. It seems like I knew you so long ago but then just yesterday, if you can follow me. Right now I simply don't understand what I am thinking."

"You've got that one right, Madison. I'm told you have amnesia, so the fact that you remember me is an important step to improving."

"Are you married? Oh, why did I ask that? I'm being pushy again."

"No, never really found anyone after you, Madison, as ours was a grounding relationship for me. Maybe it was that we were so good together or maybe it was that we were too comfortable together? I don't know. I just know that I haven't found what we had since we broke up. Funny though, you never have been out of my mind, and that's one of the reasons I jumped when I received the call that you were in the hospital. Here you are teaching in Minneapolis, and I'm an engineer at the Ford plant across the river in St. Paul. I am so glad you didn't head to another state. Maybe I can continue to visit you and see you when you leave the hospital?"

"Now Dan, let's not get too carried away," commented Sandra Lee. "Your breakup was pretty tough on Madison, you know."

"Well, it's nice to know you still are in Madison's corner, Sandra. By the way, where is Madison's dad?"

"I told him to stay home, take care of Guinness and not to worry. You know how he is."

"Yes I do, Sandra. I remember Roy well. Great guy! Man's kind of a man."

"Well he would have taken you out back to the woodshed when you broke up with Madison, Mister Dan."

"Sandra, let's not go there. Madison and I were close, maybe too close back then."

"Mother, stop it! Can't you see that Dan is here out of concern for me? I bet he would not have come knowing you were here."

"Well now" huffed Sandra Lee.

"OK everybody. It's time to clear the decks. Madison is off to an MRI and will be gone for at least an hour if not more." Dr. Pike jumped in to keep her patient quiet and restful. "I suggest you all pick times best for you to visit, since Madison isn't leaving until she is back to one hundred percent." Meanwhile Dr. Pike was thinking all of this was helping Madison regain her memory faster than sitting and resting.

Dan agreed and told Madison he would be back after work, that's as long as Interstate 94 wasn't terribly busy at rush hour. Dan gave Madison a hug which lasted a bit longer than Sandra Lee expected. Visibly upset, Sandra Lee decided she would call it a day and go to her sister's house in Richfield. Madison waited for everyone to leave before she talked with Dr. Pike.

"Dr. Pike, I remember seeing a planet, OGLE-2026-BLG-1190 Lb, at the heart of the Milky Way. Sure, try those initials and numbers again. It is 22,000 light years away and is thirteen - thirteen - times greater than the size of Jupiter. It was first found by NASA's Spitzer infrared space telescope which was launched in 2003. Dr. Pike, I saw it. I really saw it! Go figure. I'm also in love with Dan, you know."

"Where did that come from, Madison? Are we focusing on a planet or on Dan?"

"I know. I know. No rhyme or reason to this conversation, is there?"

"Doesn't have to be, Madison, so just let the thoughts come out, and we can sort them out later. Having Dan in the picture makes it kind of nice for you, doesn't it?"

"Yes but I am so tired now, exhausted, Dr. Pike. Do you mind if I just take another nap for a while before the MRI?"

"A nap always is good. Go for it."

•

Dan came back; Sandra Lee waited until morning; Dr. Pike carried out other duties trusting the long rest for Madison as well as seeing Dan would be good. Dr. Pike also thought about Madison's amnesia which she hoped would not last long. She also thought about Madison's normal blood pressure, lack of muscle atrophy and skin color. Madison had been unconscious for a while but looked and acted like she hadn't been unconscious at all. Her hair was in place, and her nails were not dirty. Even her mental sharpness regarding subjects involving science couldn't have been more accurate. "How in the world does Madison know about a huge planet in the middle of the Milky Way that is ten, twelve, thirteen times the size of

Jupiter? I just read about the discovery today. And, what did she call them, muons I think, that are involved in cosmic ray imaging? Medicine doesn't even know about that. I'm almost afraid to see where all of this is taking me."

•

"Hi, Dan, you are back so soon. Is everything okay?"

"Oh yes, it's better than okay Madison, especially seeing you again."

"I probably look terrible, the accident and all, plus I haven't done anything to look or dress half way decent."

"That is the least of your worries, Madison. All you have to do now is rest, feel better and get your thoughts together. For a math major and analytical type, that shouldn't be too much to ask. Hey, I brought some new higher math, educational magazines I thought you might like. You should see some of the new equations, some of which we have been using at Ford."

"Dan, do you remember how excited we got when working on tough problems only two geeks could answer? Maybe we should have been geeks. Things might have been different."

"Things are different already, Madison. I made a big mistake by not staying with you assuming that you would have stayed with me. Who knows, we might have made it all the way to the altar."

"The altar, how did you come up with that again, the altar? Sandra Lee surely would have supported that move, and so would my dad. I would have too, Dan, and we talked about it. Trouble is you weren't ready."

"I wasn't ready, Madison, that's correct, but that doesn't mean we can't try again, I hope."

"Considering we have enjoyed talking for what, a few minutes after a long period of not knowing whether either of us were alive still, I'd say this is surely a start of sorts. Actually I'm surprised Sandra Lee didn't go after you after having hurt her little girl way back when."

"Okay, Okay, Madison. If you are throwing up barriers, Sandra Lee is a good one."

"No, I'm just talking and remembering things, thank God."

"It's a good thing, yes. So tell me what the doctor has said."

"I'm okay and am going to be okay now that I'm coming out of this amnesia thing. Dr. Pike feels your presence probably is the best thing to help me regain my memory since we were so close."

"We were, weren't we? Close that is. Being a dummy like me isn't all that easy, you know, so please know I am going to do my best to rekindle our feelings for each other."

•

"Dr Pike, I traveled past the sun, 92.96 million miles from earth. I could see the path earth takes around the sun, 584 million miles worth. It's almost like it leaves a trail of...of something. Cutting through the electromagnetic field we call space, it's like the earth and sun emit radio waves, charged particles, that carry on forever in an environment that acts only on charged particles, waves. I passed the GAIA satellite which is measuring the intensity of stars like our sun. Do you know the satellite is 115 million kilometers from earth? I also saw Hubble."

"Slow down, Madison, I can't keep up with you. How would you feel if I tried recording our conversations, since you are providing so many facts and figures that I simply can't digest very fast?"

"Of course, Dr. Pike, it's just that I have so much to say, and I don't feel I have enough time to say it. Plus I'm not sure how I retain it all. I mentioned Hubble, the Hubble telescope named after Edwin Hubble. The telescope estimates 2 trillion galaxies are out there each with billions of stars, and all having at least one planet circling it. Go figure, huh? Not only that, the galaxies furthest out there are moving away from us faster than the galaxies closer to us. Yes, I know why I'm so sure of all of this after the trip, adventure, but don't you find all of cosmology amazing as well? I'm a math teacher who loves math, but this stuff has captured my entire attention."

"Keep going, Madison. This is as fascinating to me as it is to you albeit for different reasons - but fascinating all the same. When you were talking unconsciously, you mentioned everything in the universe is either energy or matter. Sounds like old high school chemistry class information."

"It is. That is, everything in the universe is either energy or matter, and yes, that's high school science speaking, you bet. But, and it's a big 'but', I witnessed protons circling nuclei determining what kind of matter it became. Dr. Pike, that's almost like seeing the god particle except on a larger scale. After all of that, I now know the god particle sits in the light - the light at the end of the tunnel I reached before finding you talking about spinal taps."

"You mentioned gravity earlier, Madison. You said you understood gravity."

"I did, absolutely. It is made of quantum particles, waves. It isn't a force at all but rather a consequence of the curvature of space time caused by the uneven distribution of mass. How technical is that? My high school physics teachers would be impressed, I bet. And even more than that, I witnessed iron being created from stellar explosions, calcium being created from stars, and gold, yes gold, coming from merging neutron stars. Bored yet? I used to talk like this when younger, much to the chagrin of my friends and classmates. I bored them to death and wound up losing friends. I bet you understand that and also my need to slow down?"

"Madison, you are not boring me; but if we were at a cocktail party, I'd probably move to another group. Before we break, tell me again about loop quantum gravity."

"Loop quantum gravity. That's Carlo Rovelli's theory in *Seven Brief Lessons on Physics.* Rovelli postulates there is a quantum bridge between contracting and expanding cosmological branches. In other words, universes are born while others end. Dr. Pike, I saw it all. I saw universes being born as a result of quantum fluctuations as ours was 13.7 billion years ago, and I saw universes collapsing under their own weight. How do I convince anyone that I really, really did see it?"

"Let's worry about that later. Once you talk with a physicist and a theologian, you'll have an idea where all of this is going and maybe why it happened. But try it on Dan the next time you see him. If you and Dan are going to make it again as a couple, this will be a true test."

•

"Hello, Madison. I'm Rev. Anderson, Chaplain here at Fairview Southdale. I understand you are recovering from a rather nasty automobile accident. I also understand you grew up in Cottonwood, my father's home town. Do you remember the North Star Mutual Insurance Company offices, buildings I should say, on Barstad Road?"

"Hello Rev. Anderson. I certainly do remember, and I knew of the

Anderson family. Some of the kids now live in northern Minnesota, and some live as far south as Arizona. My folks knew some of the Anderson family girls. I'm guessing you are closely related."

"Yep, I'm guilty as charged. I'm the great grandson of the matriarch and grandson of his son who was president of the insurance company beginning in 1950. I grew up in a number of states moving with my dad who also was a minister. He graduated from St. Olaf; and I, Macalester in St. Paul. Both of us attended Luther Seminary in St. Paul."

"Do you know my parents?"

"No, I never lived in Cottonwood and only visited when a kid. As far Cottonwood is concerned, I find it to be one of the most wonderful towns in the country in which to raise a family, although I never got the chance myself. Call it karma if that's the right description."

"Rev. Anderson, what do you know of near death experiences? I guess I have had one, but I'm told there is so much more to what I have experienced than just near death. I witnessed it and then some, and was part of so much that I'm having trouble articulating it all."

"Well, I am here and would love to help you sort out a few things, if I can."

"Let me start with defining the origin of the Adam and Eve story. And please stop me when something doesn't sound right, although it all is. Jah and Hava, the pre-Hebraic names given to the masculine and feminine gender, Adam and Eve, according to the oral tradition of original sin dated about 3760 BCE and revised centuries later…well, that wasn't the exact date, but it is close enough, and the story itself…well, it is just that, a story. You know that, and you know the Jewish calendar takes us to 5778 today. You also know the story of Abraham whether a real person, a tribe by the name of Abraham or just an oral tradition passed down from tribe to tribe. Rev. Anderson, I saw the beginning; I felt I was there; I saw it much like it was an old Movietone newsreel. I became part of the entire lineage from Jah and Hava to Noah to Nimrod to Abraham to Moses to David to Jesus. By part of, I mean I saw it like a bystander, observing everything. But at the same time I saw Confucius and Buddha both in the 5th Century BCE. My God, Rev. Anderson, I even saw Mohammed later in 631 CE."

"Madison, you have my attention, but how did all of this happen? I'll have to study near death experiences, but I doubt that will answer how this revelation came to you."

"Reverend, I saw Raphael, Michael, Gabriel and even Uriel and Jeremiel from the *Jewish Apocrypha.* I listened to Thomas Aquinas define the angels as being 'completely spiritual, no mineral, vegetal or animal substances - an intellectual nature that assumed bodies. Angels can be anywhere successively.' Rev. Anderson the Apostles experiences were as horrible as we have read. Simon Peter was crucified upside down; Andrew's brother Simon, was crucified; James was beheaded. And then there was Augustine, Saint Augustine, telling us suffering, the existence of evil is a conflict between free will and the omnipresent divine. 'Good and bad things happen to the righteous and the wicked.' You know all of this, I'm sure, but I have so much to say that I am growing anxious and uneasy about this moment in our conversation."

"I understand, so let's break for a while. If this is helpful, Madison, you have to let me know before we go on further. As a Christian, I like everything you say. It's just that...just that it is almost impossible, unreal to grasp. I used the word unreal rather than anything that would put doubt into your description of what happened for a purpose. I am a very accepting person, and I want to know more. You may be on the verge of telling us something we need to know. Tomorrow works then?"

"Tomorrow then, yes. Thank you, and please take note of one last thing. I am becoming an advocate of Karl Barth who believed 'Existential theology demands faith be individual. Faith is not found in organized religions, rituals or texts.' Everything I have experienced tells me this."

•

"Still tired, Madison? Looks like you slept for better than a couple of hours. Not only that, but you sent Rev. Anderson out talking to himself. He asked if I had any information on near death experiences. He is a great guy, family man and supporter of all we do at the hospital, plus he is Lutheran which doesn't hurt in this State of Norwegians and Swedes. I have a feeling he'll be ready to talk a bit more the next time he visits if it isn't too much out of his comfort level. How are you feeling right now? Seems like you are getting your memory back?"

"Dr. Pike, have you read anything by Martin Buber? He refers to Jewish existentialism in this way. 'In the encounter with God as the individual hears Him speaking in the deepest recesses of one's being, each hears what he can hear and obeys that which he personally heard.' Dr. Pike, I think that is what has occurred in my life. The more I sit and wonder, the more I can accept the trip, the adventure, I was on was a direct encounter with God. I reached the light - yes, yes the light at the end of the tunnel - but was turned back for some reason. Could it be that I have something to say? Could it be that I am not alone in experiencing this? Could it be that I have to find someone who has experienced the same?"

"You are moving too fast for me again. Slooooow down. Buber is the 'existence is encounter' guy. By that I mean every day we encounter God just by being. Your experience certainly is in the category of 'existence is encounter' but I don't know that it is you and you alone. What you have told me pretty well convinces me you had an experience unlike that of anyone before you - anyone. You have scanned billions of years in what appears to be, as you called it, a picosecond. Why that picosecond didn't equate to hundreds even thousands of years on earth, I don't know. Maybe it's not for me or you to know either. If your adventure as you call it, brought you back full-circle to Minneapolis, there has to be a reason. I just hope I can help you find that reason."

"Dr. Pike, it was Karl Barth who said 'It is reasonable to suppose that there are no higher intelligences than ourselves in the universe until we reach the level of God.' You know something? I was so close to the light and being able to address that comment in an intelligent and educated way. Barth also said 'Existential theology demands faith be individual. Faith is not found in organized religions, rituals or texts.' Well, I found it, that's for sure.

Here is another thing, Dr. Pike, I could not have quoted Martin Buber or Karl Barth before my adventure. Sure, I had heard their names and probably read something about them, but they aren't standard fare for mathematicians."

"Go on, Madison, this exercise is proving so very valuable for you - and me too. How you can quote anything at all after your concussion is amazing."

"For example, take the Dane, Soren Kierkegaard, he addressed questions of meaning and life as they affected individuals. That's me, an individual woman who has no idea how to handle life after this thing I'm calling an adventure. The poor guy died at age 42 of a broken heart in 1855."

"Who, Madison? Who told you that? Answer quickly, whatever name comes to mind. This is an important step."

"The light told me. It was the light. My God I remember now. Dr. Pike, I did hear voices after all. Sure I saw everything and knew what was being said almost by osmosis - no, a supreme consciousness, if that's good term to use. But the light told me so many more things… so many more things."

"Don't stop now. Let's take this further."

"I remember Reinhold Niebuhr saying 'Ethics are worthless unless they tell us how to change the immediate environment for the better.' That's Christian Realism. Is that what I am doing, Dr. Pike, going through these memories in order to help man change for the better? Who said, let me think a sec. Who said 'Humans and the universe are inseparable'? Sure, it was Pierre Teilhard de Chardin in the 20th Century. I think I am living proof that humans and the universe are inseparable. Wow! What could possibly be next?"

"How about a little rest, Madison? That should be next, since you are moving with lightning speed which is challenging for you as well as for me. I need a rest too, and I still have rounds to make on the floor. Let's take a break."

"Okay, but one last thing this session, and that is Kierkegaard wrote 'Life can be understood backwards, but it must be lived forwards.' I'm doing it, Dr. Pike, living it forward after the adventure.

"Go to sleep, Madison."

•

"Do you remember the amount of time we spent in the library, even necking in the darker study areas, the carrels? Think we could ever go there again - to that kind of feeling for each other, I mean? I have been working at Ford totally remiss of any kind of social life, outside life, fun except for seeing old classmates once and awhile. As soon as I received the call about your accident, I realized how much I have missed you and maybe the family about which we talked more than a few times. As a matter of fact, I have led a very dull life since college. What's that all about?"

"Me too, Dan, dull, really dull when it comes to anything but my students. Other than working and visiting Cottonwood on vacations, I haven't had much of a social life myself. Of course, spending too much time with Sandra Lee could make one dull anyway. Do I think we could start anew? Yes. Do I think it will be the same? No, but that's good. You have changed and so have I. Now all we can do is try I guess."

"Terrific! I want to do it too. Now how can I help you get back to normal."

"Dan, you need to know what just happened to me. I think I came to God's door - his real door and not just a church door in Bloomington. I'm told I died and then came back to life. Rather than question all of that, I have been remembering all the things that happened to me when I was clinically dead. No, I haven't been 'born again' and haven't been watching evangelical TV. I took a trip, an adventure of sorts, that I need to sort through with the help of Dr. Pike, maybe Rev. Anderson and hopefully you. I know who God is. He is simple - no parts. He is perfect - complete. He is infinite - not finite in any way. He is immutable incapable of change and He is one. Those are the words of Thomas Aquinas in *Summa Theologica*. No need to ask me how I know all that right now, I just do. Kind of crazy, huh? What's just as crazy is that I'd love to have you hold me close. I need that. How's that for a suggestion?"

"Your wish is my command, Madison. I am liking this."

•

"Rev. Anderson, I'm pretty well versed in the precepts of John Calvin. His ideas about predestination, original sin, and salvation of some and not others wouldn't fly where I have been in the last...I don't know how long. Even Islam doesn't accept the concept of original sin. Trouble is Calvin succeeded Martin Luther in prominence not just in Germany or France but also in conservative thought everywhere. Where I have been doesn't account for that. It would seem humanity was created immature and continues to mature. John Hick, *Evil and the Love of God*, wrote that his philosophy is just that. Furthermore Hick says that death is not evil, as some think. It is how we come to know God. I'm there with him, Rev. Anderson. Not only that, but I have been there and back. Go figure, huh?"

"Madison, you are a level above me in your understanding of theology, and I'm impressed. I don't have any question that you need to meet with some of the faculty at Luther Seminary."

"That would be great, and we can start with my thoughts about interpreting all of my experiences, although I might shake their beliefs to their foundations. That's okay since the reality of death will confront them someday anyway. Even Rabbi Harry Kushner, *Jewish Spirituality,* believes we are living in the continuous presence of the divine. I believe that is the light I reached, and I just didn't know until right now that the light is always there."

•

"Mother, what do you know about Carl Jung?"

"Who is Carl Jung? Madison, you are scaring me. I couldn't talk with your brother, and now I'm beginning to feel I can't talk with you. Maybe it's time I had your father come up to Edina and the hospital."

"That's it, Mom! You are feeling; you are intuitive; you are thinking. Remember years ago when you took aptitude tests? That's what it's about. Where do your interests lie? So the tests were to point out. You remember those, I hope. The framework of those tests was structured by Carl Jung."

"You are talking down to me, Madison. I don't like that. And yes, of course I remember taking those tests. Neither your father nor I felt they were that helpful in that we knew what we wanted. Your dad wanted to build a career selling like your grandfather, and I wanted to raise a big family. Five children later along with a very successful manufacturer rep company, and here we are."

"Mother, you and Roy were nothing but a success story doing all of that. I don't mean to talk down to you or anyone. It's just that I'm having trouble putting my thoughts together, and I wanted to talk more about Jung."

"Well hello, Sandra Lee and Madison. How are we doing today?"

"We are doing quite well, Doctor, except Madison is on a tangent causing me a great deal of concern"

"Let me deal with that, Sandra Lee. Your daughter has just come through a severe concussion as well as amnesia both of which will make her confused. No time to judge her, for sure. A little time will heal everything."

"Doctor, she looks fine to me. Maybe she would be best in Cottonwood recovering with her father and me?"

"What a wonderful idea! Let her rest here a while and heal those internal injuries, and then Cottonwood might be a good choice. You do look good, Madison, and your mother means well. Let's give this a few more days. OK?"

"Thank you, Dr. Pike. I need to rest more; I can feel it."

"Good. Let me call you father and tell him you are getting much better and will be coming home. I guess I can't see your internal injuries."

•

"Dr. Pike, Immanuel Kant wrote in his *Critique of Pure Reason*, 'It is impossible to extend knowledge to the supersensible realm of speculative physics. That is because our knowledge is constrained to mathematics and science of the natural, empirical world.' That's not an exact quote, of course, but the point I need to make is that I think I have gone beyond the constraints. Yes, I understand him now. Yes, I'm convinced I have gone beyond the constraints.

Kant also believed that there was a supreme principle of morality which he referred to as the Categorical Imperative. 'An action's status is morally good if it is commanded by God.' His moral theory was based on his view of the human being as having the unique capacity for rationality. I think he was correct.

And by the way, Dr. Pike, thank you for holding off my mother."

"You are something else, Madison. Challenge me in science, I love that. But your understanding of theology and philosophy is away from me as it seems to be for Rev. Anderson. He is holding his chapel service in the hospital later this week, and I suggest you and I attend. I'm wondering if some of what you have said will be included in his homily. The man is more of a pastor than an intellectual, is my guess. You just might have provided him some new insights that will benefit his work with patients here. And you are welcome, by the way. That's part of my job - fending off controlling parents when it comes to misunderstanding medicine and healing."

"I agree. He already has suggested I meet with some of the faculty at Luther Seminary in St. Paul. I certainly am not a theologian or philosopher, Dr. Pike, so what am I getting myself into here?"

"You have alluded to that question before, Madison. I suggest we let happen what will happen. Your trip - adventure - was for a reason, and we need to determine what that reason is. Maybe the answer will be easier to figure out than we think? I'd like to think it is right before our eyes."

•

"Good morning. I always am happy to see so many of the hospital's patients and staff for our mid-week, non-denominational chapel service. All of us ask for help from somewhere at some time in life - I like to think it is God we are asking - when pressure builds on the job as well as when pain seems unrelenting and unstoppable.

The *Bible* verse we read a few moments ago always is appropriate for in-hospital homilies of this nature especially when we recognize how simple the verse is. 'Pain results in suffering; suffering causes us to endure; endurance builds character; and character is a basis for hope.' Is there any question all of us come together with a hope that someday the entity some of us call God will provide us the answer for all that we experience in life, good and bad?

I must admit my faith has been strengthened this week meeting with patients. I have been challenged to look more closely at what happens when we die. How do we get to heaven? When does one go to hell? Where is heaven or hell? Is our simplistic view of heaven up above and hell down below too simplistic? Of course it is. But then, what is the correct view?

One of our patients recently told me that Ian Barbour, a retired religion and physics professor just south of us at Carleton College in Northfield wrote 'If we take the *Bible* seriously but not literally, we can accept the central Biblical message without accepting the pre-scientific cosmology in which it was expressed such as the three layered universe with heaven above and hell below, or the seven day creation story.'

It would seem to me that we are learning the answers ever so slowly - almost at the limit of our capacity to understand. That makes sense to me. Actually I think of myself as living in a transparent box from which I cannot escape. Everything tangible is in that box with me. I can eat, sleep, work, raise a family, play and enjoy those aspects of life provided me. However, outside that transparent box lie answers to questions I cannot answer while inside. Who am I? Why am I here? Where am I going? These are the questions mankind has been asking since the beginning.

So the challenge I issue to myself is that I study near death experiences more closely; I look at quantum mechanics to see if there is anything there God is telling us; and finally, I draw together thoughts of educated men on the topic of death. It would seem they have provided some answers that we haven't accepted fully yet."

•

At that point Madison began to grow tired. Dr. Pike recognized it and nudged Madison to sneak out the back of the chapel.

"He believes you, Madison. Your conversations have elevated his thoughts from that of a chaplain to more of a theologian. Interesting isn't it? Young woman dies or experiences a near death event, talks about it so articulately that a medical doctor, me, and an ordained chaplain, Rev. Anderson, have to take note and do something about it. Now I ask you, what's that all about?"

"Dr. Pike, I have something to say, and I know now for sure what it is. It's just going to take me a while longer to verbalize it, although the idea of being in a transparent box appeals to me. Also Dr. Pike, I'm going to reach a bit here by suggesting that maybe, after all, I did die and not just have a near death experience. Doesn't that throw a wrench in the gears, huh? I am beginning to feel I died, traveled to the light at the end of whatever I was inside, experienced the impact of the light as I've suggested to you, and now am back to share the experience with others. What do you think?"

"Too early for me to tell, and that's if I'm in a position to say anyway. Maybe it will take physics professors, scientists and theologians to figure this out after all."

"Dr. Pike, I have seen the evolution of Rev. Anderson's Christian faith. I have seen the four stages including orthodoxy, oriental Christianity, western Catholicism and Protestantism; and I probably understand it better than most. I have seen the rudiments of the Torah written centuries before Christ. I know the questions about which Rev. Anderson is talking - and the answers. The answer is in the light towards which we all are moving. Now you can tell me I'm crazy. It won't surprise me at all."

"Madison, you are crazy! Feel better? Please don't ask that again. Okay? Of course you are not crazy, because people who push the envelope, go out on a limb, or rattle some cages always are considered crazy or different. In your case you have had an experience very few, if any, have ever had. And let me tell you, you are about to do those very things - push, go out and rattle - believe me."

"I know. I know so much, it seems. I was there when Irenaeus of Lyons declared all but the four, true *Gospels* were not acceptable as early as 180 CE. Maybe I should say I saw Irenaeus make that declaration. Funny, it led to the burying of the other books including the *Gnostic Gospels* along the Upper Nile by the Pachomian Monks who feared their books would be destroyed. That was in the 4rd Century CE, would you believe? What influence the old boys had, and it wasn't just Irenaeus. Another Bishop by the name of Athanasius squashed most other books about Christ and early Christianity, and he was one of the leading architects of Christianity at the Council of Nicaea in 324 CE. Are you still comfortable with all of this, Dr. Pike?"

"Oh, I'm comfortable alright, yes, but let's get back to the trip, the adventure."

"Hard to sort out my thoughts, since they keep coming, flooding my mind. Hopefully the sorting is difficult because of my amnesia which seems to be less and less of a problem. Dr. Pike, I can go on and on, as you know, and as long as it is beneficial."

"It is beneficial, Madison. Let's say you did reach the light; let's say you answered the question no one has been able to answer since the beginning of time; let's say you did come back to tell us - mankind. Let's say you and only you know where we are going when we die. Then let's figure out the best way to share that with people who need to know. That's the tough part, Madison. How in the world do we tell people what you know without labeling you a candidate for the psychiatric ward? We have addressed that question before, so now we need to get down to specifics. And Madison, you need to know that I believe you. That is important, and I think our friend, Rev. Anderson, believes you as well."

"Let me tell you about the *Theory of Neo-Biocentrism* and how I feel about it. That's the Robert Lanza theory you told me I mentioned when I was unconscious. In a nutshell, Lanza states we identify ourselves with our body. 'We created time and space to explain our animal sense of perception, and we carry time and space around like a turtle shell. Because consciousness exists outside of the constraints of time and space which are not physical objects, death is an illusion in our minds because of that very fact we identify with our bodies.' That is me, Dr. Pike. My body died - you told me so. My heart shut down, and blood stopped flowing to my brain. But I continued to think and exist outside my physical body. Even Michael Angelo who convinced us that the moon reflects the sun in 1490, said 'The center of the brain is the seat of the soul where all parts come together.' He couldn't have known that through any scientific method back then, but he did know it; and now I, a middle school math teacher, can prove it.

Dr. Pike, I am the embodiment of theoretical physics. I don't know why, but I have proven the theories of general relativity, quantum mechanics, particle physics, cosmology, quantum gravity, the arrow of time and consciousness. Maybe it is because I know how to employ mathematical models and abstractions of physical objects to explain natural phenomena."

"Time to shut it down again, Madison. I can't take notes fast enough and my phone isn't recording. What do you think of my bringing in some experts in the fields of theology and science, maybe as soon as we talk again?"

"Please, let's do it. Outstanding idea!"

•

"Rev. Anderson, how are you today?"

"Very good, thank you, but the real question is how are you? Dr. Pike tells me you are improving faster than expected and are ready to 'wow' both of us again. What have you been doing since I last saw you in chapel? Are you thinking of spending time in Cottonwood with Sandra Lee?"

"To be honest I've been thinking of spending time in bed with Dan in St. Paul soon. We had a terrific sex life once, and both of us miss it."

"That sounds great, Madison, but it probably is not a good idea to share that with Sandra Lee."

"Rev. Anderson, I witnessed the development of the West Bank, and it was not easy as you might think. When the 12 tribes moved south they went to Judea, now Jerusalem. The territory later went to the Babylonians, then the Persians, and the Greeks and Romans. I was there when the Balfour Declaration was written and enacted in 1917 allowing the Jews to build a homeland in Palestine – the former Canaan, Philista. Then the Jewish State was established in 1948. Finally we see it cut up the way it has been since 1967 Six Day War. Ever wonder why God let it happen that way?"

"Madison, you cut to the quick very fast. God doesn't intervene in earthly matters the way we would like. Never has. I suppose the great flood, the Tower of Babel, Moses leaving Egypt, and the birth of Christ indicate to some God interfered at times, but don't ask him to win a football game. That stuff doesn't count. He gave us freewill, Madison. It is up to us."

"Good points but no cigar, Chaplain. He, she or whatever has put in place what I call 'Project Humanity' has left it up to us to make things work and go smoothly, although we have proven that to be all but impossible. All we can do - all - is to carry on with good Judeo/Christian, Buddhist, Islamic, Hindu, or Shinto values working to make life better for all. Then we can expect to take the last great adventure and meet the source of it all, God, the Lawmaker, the source of energy itself. I know because I have been there; I know because I have taken the adventure; and equally important is that I know how we get to the source, the light. Now all I have to figure out is why I am back."

•

"Good morning, everyone, I really am not that comfortable being here, but Rev. Anderson tells me that is a normal reaction. I never have met with a group of theologians before other than attending special church services or shaking hands with a Bishop in Minneapolis. However, Dr. Pike, who already has been introduced, has joined me as a mentor. As you know, she is an M.D. as well as a PhD Psychiatrist, and she is my guide through all of this - and there is a lot of this to guide me through.

Rev. Anderson was correct when he said I was looking for an answer to why I returned from what some call a near death experience. I do not have the background to question the assumption of a near death experience, but I do know that mine was more than just that. I reached the end of a tunnel, a wormhole, a conduit to a light which is mentioned in so many near death experiences. Yes, I reached it, felt it, heard it, touched it and recognized it as the answer to the third great metaphysical question, where am I going after death? I know the answer is not as simple as heaven or hell. I believe you do as well."

"Madison, I think it is wonderful that you are here today. As Dean of the Religion Department, I am fascinated by all you told Rev, Anderson. While you search for your answer, I'll be searching for mine, that being, how did you gain such intimate knowledge of church history? Unless you are a closet scholar, you couldn't have assimilated so much by happenstance."

"Dean, Baruch Spinoza wrote 'Our clear knowledge of God and God's Will increases in proportion to our knowledge and clear understanding of nature. Since God and nature are the same thing, therefore the mind and the body are two aspects of the same thing. All exists as one substance, the mental and the physical are different attributes of that one substance.' Dean, I feel I am living proof of that statement. I experienced all of nature on my adventure, and I almost touched God.

Zhang Xianliang wrote in *Getting Used to Dying* that 'Dying is not so simple. We normally achieve it only once in a lifetime.' Yes, that is humorous.

For those of you who do not know of him, he wrote of his experiences in China from 1936 onward. Members of the faculty here at Luther, I already have died, and believe me that I know I am not another Sun God or Jesus Christ or anything like that. I am a Midwest math teacher who was hit by an automobile sending me on an adventure unlike anything out there. But why...why did I return?

Do you remember reading *The Egyptian Book of the Dead*? Maybe not, I don't know. But I do know that Egyptians believed, that rising from the body's entombed remains, a spiritual body would emerge. Interestingly they believed the heart was the center of spiritual feeling. All of that was drafted in 2000 - 1500 BCE in a collection of ancient writings which referred to the afterlife. I now know they were correct in the sense that one's spirit, one's soul, one's consciousness does emerge from death, although not quite the way they thought.

Now, here is where we are going to have trouble understanding each other. I am living proof of consciousness existing after death of the physical body. Not easy to digest is it, especially with my physical presence here today.

Did you know Marcus Aurelius wrote that the plan of the universe was for man to return to the primeval fire of all things into which all beings will eventually fall? His was an assumption, of course. But he was so very close especially without the help of science to further his argument. Think about it. He wrote *Meditations* sometime before his death in 180 CE. That's 180 CE! What did man know about science then, and how much closer could he have been to what I have experienced?"

"Madison, I think you will find the subject of death addressed many times by theologians worldwide who understand science. As an example, even today I'm not comfortable with the Seventh Day Adventist who expects the dead to sleep until the return of Jesus Christ."

"Yes, yes, you are on the right track, Dean. The Seventh Day Adventist will say a spirit does not enter heaven of hell immediately upon death. My spirit, my consciousness certainly didn't enter either, but it did not sleep. That is why I am looking for an answer."

"Are you a Seventh Day Adventist, Madison? To us it would appear so."

"No, I'm Catholic, a Roman Catholic, and we really do not have any statement regarding near death experiences. Catholics have had near death experiences, of course, but the Church has stayed out of the discussion about them."

"How do you know that, Madison?"

"Ready for this, Dean? Because I was there participating from a distance - akin to an out of body experience. As I turn and look at Rev. Anderson who I brought into this discussion a short time ago, I realize this stuff is so very hard to accept. But how else would I know it if I were not there? Again I say I am not a theologian or *Bible* thumper."

"One last comment before we all have to break, I assume you believe in God, Jesus Christ and the Holy Spirit?"

"Dean, I do but for different reason than you. There is something else out there that we cannot comprehend yet, although I now believe God is leading us to a better understanding of it all. Even Confucius believed in the existence of a supreme being, a supreme cosmic spiritual power, and Confucius accepted some sort of existence after death. Surely that is one of the reasons he promoted - promoted is not the best word, I'm sure - his Golden Rule. And that was in the 5th Century BCE."

•

"Hi Madison, I'm told you are ready to head home."

"Dan, I am but not to Cottonwood, and let me tell you how that is going to go over with Sandra Lee. Roy will be okay with my decision, but I can hear Sandra Lee already."

"Yep, so where are you going?"

"To my apartment in Richfield, want to come?"

"Richfield, huh? Oh, yes, absolutely yes. How...I get it. No car means Dan lucked out and gets to go to your apartment."

"Kind of like that, although you might be surprised what you find there."

"Just tell me it will not be Sandra Lee."

"I wouldn't do that to you, ever."

•

"Dr. Pike, where do we go from here? Fortunately I'm only minutes away on the Crosstown Highway from Richfield."

"I office both here and at the Doctor's Office Park on Lynndale close to Richfield. Remember the drill, Madison. Write down all that you remember, and then bring it to our discussions - which, by the way, should be at least three times a week. The insurance company of the driver who hit you will cover the cost."

"So what do you think after having listened to me when unconscious and now conscious? How difficult is it to believe me?"

"Madison, you are in a league of your own. Your question 'Why did I come back?' may never be answered, but something will surface to give you a better understanding of what happened. Just be careful of anyone who professes to know the answer, since you know full well there are too many charlatans out there who would love to make money off your story. Listen to what the Dean and the faculty said at Luther. They probed and probed. That's the best response."

"And what about Dan?"

"That's away from me, but if it were me, I'd go for it. Your reconnecting after a few years is great, plus he is a very nice guy. Even your mother said that, and that's something. Plus I think jumping in bed with him again may allow you to relax more. However, you did catch Rev. Anderson off guard with that statement."

"I like Rev. Anderson a lot, speaking of nice guys. My comment was an honest one not meant to shock him.'

"He knows that, but he has been away from down to earth talk for a while."

•

"Dan, what do you think of the transfiguration on Mt. Hermon when God spoke to Peter, James, John and Jesus alongside Moses and Elijah? "

"Madison, I don't have a clue. I haven't even thought about it for a long, long time."

"That's OK. Have you ever heard of the 'thin space' between heaven and earth? That's when an angel of the Lord approached Mary Magdalene at the tomb of Jesus saying 'Do not be afraid' - same phrase God used at the transfiguration."

"I love you, Madison. That's what I think. You remind me of the kid I knew in the library, but you are too much for me right now."

"You are good, Dan, the same old Dan I knew so long ago. This time, however, your assignment is to help me put the pieces of the puzzle together - not unlike figuring out some of those math formulas.

But how does God communicate with us? The concept of a sovereign, eternal being that created the universe and confining itself to a human body was, and is, too much for some people to believe. But how else could he communicate with us? How does he communicate with us today beyond even that 'thin place'?

Dan, I'm getting it; I'm getting it right now! He communicates with us through experiences like mine. De Chardin wrote 'There is a unity in which the collective and the individual come into fruition and are perfected, unity in God in which the world becomes divinized filled with the divine presence.'

Dan, I'm getting there, yes, to the answer of my question. The book of *Ecclesiastes* reads 'Everything has its time.' The key word is time - time as we know it. The Apostle Paul put it this way in *2 Corinthians*, 'So we fix our eyes not on what is seen, but on what is unseen. For what we see is temporary, but what is unseen is eternal.' Hey, I am not an evangelist or a Jesus freak, just a young math teacher. But what I am learning is that I experienced something that addresses Paul's comments as well as those in *Ecclesiastes*.

Then there is 'Let there be light!' Light! How in the world did Moses and the writers of Genesis come up with that? Talk about thinking outside the box. The Big Bang was the light. Maybe I should say lights rather than light. Hans Durr said there is not a [one] Big Bang…it happens all the time."

"How about a nap, Madison, what do you think? Let's see what happens when we snuggle again. We have a lot more to catch up on now that we are back together, and I'm having trouble staying with all your thoughts."

•

"Mother wasn't happy, isn't happy I should say; but she is coming to Richfield anyway with Roy, I think. Dan is okay with it, of course. He has changed, Dr. Pike, and for the better."

"Let's review your notes, Madison. I'm interested in what you have discovered."

"Great! Let's talk quantum mechanics for a change. I have determined that an elementary and fundamental particle, a constituent of matter must hold memory, my memory, my consciousness, and my soul if that is what we prefer to call it. Possibly it is a quark which when combined forms hadrons, the most stable of which are protons and neutrons. Three quarks form a qubit, you know what they are, quantum bits. Those quarks, maybe even qubits, when unbalanced result in an instantaneous transmission across light years of distance to find its source. My consciousness was in a quark or qubit. Is this too much for you, Dr. Pike?"

"No, absolutely, since I have done some homework on the subject which makes me think you could be accurate about your adventure or your assumption, at the least. But here is a question for you. From what I have read, the passage to the source of energy and back may be instantaneous for you, but for those left behind, it might be years. Why didn't your adventure bring you back years after you left?"

"From what I understand, Dr. Pike, I travelled faster than the speed of light both to and from, which means I moved backwards in time when returning. If that is correct I could have or actually did come back to Minneapolis about the same time I left. That also may answer why I felt different when I first came out of amnesia and felt my body. It was all there, but it felt different and caused me to question myself - almost like having jet lag on a severe basis and not just amnesia.

Space and time are not dynamic, Dr. Pike, but both ripple like the surface of a pond. That's from Stephen Hawking, and it is applicable to my adventure. I felt the ripple effect.

So now I have something to say that really might shock you. I feel compelled to go back, back to the light; I'm beginning to think I belong there."

"I was wondering when you might say that, Madison. I am not certain of the cause at this time, but you seem to be experiencing the Stockholm syndrome. You have developed a psychological alliance with the light. Whatever power is in the light has captured you - entirely."

•

"It's wonderful to be back on the Olaf campus, Dr. Treon. Your return email was more than I expected, and your willingness to see me so fast is very much appreciated. Thank you. As you know, I was not and am not a physics student. Math was my first love, and teaching math must be my second - other than my renewed relationship with Dan who you remembered in your email. We used to walk the bridges in the Arb over at Carleton and go down to the Cannon River when the water was high. We loved spring here in Northfield on campus in Norway Valley and Heath Creek even though we had to spend so much time in the Olaf library."

"Madison, go on with your email thoughts on neutrinos. How did you know it was CERN that first found them?"

"Dr. Treon, CERN was having problems with measurements due to an unforeseen and previously unmeasured element, particle, in the universe. Of course that is the neutrino about which we have communicated. They have no charge and have little or no mass and were created in less than a second following the Big Bang. They also have been proven to move faster than the speed of light. It is the most abundant particle in the universe, is not affected by electromagnetic or strong forces, and interacts with weak subatomic force and gravity while remaining electrically neutral. A neutrino is a fermion much like neutral leptons are neutrinos. Yes, they truly are the most abundant particle in the universe, and trillions of them pass through us each second mostly from the sun and other bodies in the universe. Of course they are components of everything.

Dr. Treon, I saw them being created at the time of the Big Bang, and I witnessed CERN struggling to find the particle causing it problems."

"Madison, I'm happy to talk with you about neutrinos, but that last statement is a bit much. How did you see them being created?"

"I was there. I also was there when multiple universes were created. Stephen Hawking and Carlo Rovelli wrote of multiple universes. Dr. Treon, I died not that long ago. I found myself heading towards a light while passing through time and space and the universe as we know them. Dr. Treon, I..."

"Madison, we have to stop here. Physics works only when we can prove a theory, otherwise all is speculation, and you are speculating without any proven ability to quantify your statements. That's not the way I think, and that is not an acceptable hypothesis in my field of study. Your knowledge of neutrinos, however, is amazingly accurate for a non-physicist, but I am so sorry everything else does not sit well with me."

"Dr. Treon, you are wonderful. Thank you. You have allowed me to further limit the disciplines in which I can study my experiences. What I have gone through simply is not believable or acceptable to 99.9999 percent of mankind, so somehow I am going to have to find a method to prove that which I know is true. Wish me luck, please."

"Madison, certainly I wish you luck, but first you have to make sure you understand why you know so much about the universe, consciousness and even neutrinos. That information came from somewhere. I'm at a loss to say where."

•

"Dan, I have run into too many roadblocks already. I believe religion in today's environment can't accept my story because it threatens them. Physics will never accept my story unless I can prove in a formula what happened.

Dr. Pike is so accepting and non-judgmental, but even she can't help. What would you suggest I do now, Dear Dan?"

"You said it once before Madison that the answer will take time. "Everything has its time" you said when quoting the *Bible*. We might have to sit this one out for a while. Meanwhile we have a lot to do. First, we have our jobs, then we have to deal with Sandra Lee. You have multiple meetings coming up with Dr. Pike and then others in various disciplines, and who knows, you just might find it time to visit my folks. We have to decide where this relationship is going and then maybe move in together or just get married. I can only imagine what kind of a mother you will be. How about those for starters?

PART THREE

The Last Great Adventure

THE LAST GREAT ADVENTURE

Part Three
The Last Great Adventure

"Sandra Lee, how nice it is to see you. When did you get into town?"

"Last night, Dan, it's nice to see you too. Roy decided to stay in Cottonwood, so I caught up with my sister again on the airport side of Richfield. I could have come right over, but it was getting late. Plus I didn't know you were here, so it's a good thing I didn't, huh? So where is Madison?"

"We would love to have had you here, Sandra Lee, you know that. I'm not sure where Madison has gone. She was out by the time I got up, and she didn't leave a message. That's not like her, but she is recovering from amnesia, so who knows?"

"You know she is not coming back to Cottonwood with me, Dan. Are you the reason?"

"I wish I were, Sandra. Seems she has a number of reasons for staying in Minneapolis, and she hasn't been able to tell me every one yet. It's the head injury, no question."

"Maybe that's why she isn't coming to Cottonwood after all - the head injury, of course."

"Look at it this way Sandra, she is going to meet with Dr. Pike three days a week to start. Then she has booked any number of appointments with history and science teachers and local priests. Her schedule takes her into the evening every day of the next couple of weeks which is going to be exhausting for her."

"That's another reason for coming to Cottonwood - rest. What about her job security?"

"As good as it always has been. I think everyone was so surprised when I called and said she decided she would go back to work as fast as she could. She loves the kids, and they, of course, will be thrilled she will not be gone long."

"Dan, what do you really know about near death experiences?"

"Boy, that's the question of the month in my life. What I know is that studies of people who have had near death experiences tell us one's essence, being, soul, mind, and consciousness immediately move to another dimension through a tunnel to… to wherever the light is in a near death experience - maybe the same light that is in Madison's experience. An individual's thoughts, senses, feelings and intuition may be captured in a wave or wavelet that has been proven by science not to be governed by the laws of physics. That wave or wavelet can move at the speed of light or many times faster. Sound like Madison?

Science, religion and philosophy have provided many answers to the first two great metaphysical questions, who am I and why am I here? However, neither science nor religion has provided a definitive answer to the third great metaphysical question, where am I going? Then again, science, most specifically the science of quantum mechanics, may have provided an answer to how we get to… to wherever we are going. Maybe Madison did find out?"

"Dan, how can we accept all of that? Even Madison's dad is going to question its feasibility."

"Try this, Sandra Lee. Raymond Moody, MD, PhD, author of *Life Ever After*, once wrote 'One of the nine elements that generally occur during a near death experience is the tunnel experience. This involves being drawn into a tunnel, at an extremely high speed, until reaching a radiant golden-white light.' Moody lists the experiences this way - a tunnel experience or entering darkness, a rapid movement towards a powerful light, heightened senses, out-of-body experiences, feelings of peace and quiet, coming to a border or limit, and worldwide consistencies with the experience."

"I still don't understand, Dan. How can that happen?"

"Again, that is the question of the month or year, maybe lifetime for me. However, it is documented, and that's all I know along with Madison telling us the same."

"Should I wait for her, Dan?"

Absolutely, you bet. She has coffee on the counter and cable in the other room. Kind of a nice apartment, Sandra Lee, and her taste is pretty good."

"She gets that from me, you know, and not her father whose favorite decorations are out of the 50s - aluminum and vinyl chairs, even lava lamps. I love that man, but…"

"Before I go, Sandra Lee, let me cite one other thing I learned about near death experiences. Jeffrey Long, M.D. writes in his book, *God and the Afterlife,* that crystal clear consciousness, heightened senses, perfect playback, and realistic out-of-body experiences are almost uniformly accurate in every detail in near death experiences. Some see a bright light; others go through a tunnel; still others experience a review of their life. 'I looked up and saw this light; it wasn't a normal light. It was different. I went into this tunnel…' Who does that sound like?"

•

"Dr. Pike, this is Dan. Have you heard from Madison today? She left her apartment in Richfield early this morning and didn't leave a note as to her whereabouts, and I'm beginning to get concerned."

"Hi Dan, I have no idea where she is. In fact, she missed her appointment with me this morning - first time for her. That doesn't sound like the person I know especially since she didn't call. How about you, are you calling from St. Paul?"

"I am, yes. I have been at the plant since nine when my shift started. Sandra Lee probably is still at Madison's apartment since she stopped in around 8:00 AM this morning. She was in OK spirits considering she found me at the apartment while thinking I must have been the reason her daughter didn't go to Cottonwood. Nice of her, huh? I let the comment go without upsetting her further. You know the woman drives me nuts."

"I'll talk with Madison about that when I see her next. Anyway, Dan, where do you think she went?"

"I checked at school, and she isn't there otherwise I wouldn't have called you. She had lined up so many appointments with academic types that I decided not to write them all down, so who knows where she went? I'll keep trying to find her when I am on break."

"Dan, one thing you should know, as it relates to Madison's mind. I have been reading this. The behavior of consciousness is akin to the behavior of an electron in and out of an atom. The electron, which is a quantum entity, a wave or wavelet, can remain localized inside an atom by quantum mechanical interaction with the electromagnetic field around the nucleus, which itself is quantum in nature so long as the energy of the quantum state the atom occupies matches the energy possessed by the electron. When the energy of the electron does not match, it has to shift to another state.

Consciousness may be a quantum mechanical entity that has an independent existence. It may locate in the human brain when the electron is in a particle state, and when the state changes to a wave such as at the time of death, consciousness may take flight instantaneously. That is exactly what I read about quantum mechanics of the human brain and consciousness.

That also is Madison talk, Dan, and this is what she has been saying to all of us. Dan, are you with me on this topic? This is not easy to understand."

"I am, but it worries me. How could Madison know all of this? We didn't study it at St. Olaf, and her friends never mentioned it. Madison was so into math for her kids that I can't imagine she would get into those other disciplines at the expense of losing focus of her favorite topic, that being math, of course. Something is not right here, Dr. Pike."

"Never has been right, Dan, and you know that by now. How did Madison experience an adventure like the one she described and still come back to Minneapolis in one piece? I asked her that question, but the answer can't be proven since she talks about moving faster than the speed of light. I figure it will take quite a bit of time for me to work through this with her."

"Dr. Pike, I have to run, but let me say one more thing. I found the book, *The Final Theory of God*, at Madison's apartment. You have to listen to this. Joseph B.H. McMillan, in his work, tells us science, philosophy and religion are saying the same thing but in different languages. Religion searches for a supreme law and lawmaker. Science does the same thing but calls it by a different name, energy.

McMillan writes 'We are a manifestation of the fundamental laws of the universe. Those laws are imprinted into our brains in mathematical forms which the brain then converts to words, images and forms. This is not unlike digital TV which produces forms.

McMillan who is a South African Scott, also wrote 'Morals are an example of results.'

Is this not Madison's theory? My God, the woman knows everything."

"It surely is and then some. She has been telling us that in so many words since I met her. How, I mean, where...hum, we are going to have to talk with Madison more to figure this out. Meanwhile go back to work; I have an appointment arriving. Thank you for calling, Dan, and let's keep an open line for conversations like this."

"Members of the department, as your Dean I have to admit that I am baffled by the knowledge that young lady, Madison, brought to our attention the other morning. Does anyone have any experience with Pierre de Chardine, the Jesuit, paleontologist and geologist who died in 1955? He wrote *The Phenomenon of Man* and of the Noosphere, the collective unconsciousness of humanity, the networks of thought and emotion which all are immersed.

'Evolution will culminate in the Omega Point, a supreme consciousness. Each individual fact of consciousness will remain conscious of itself at the end. From the cell to the thinking animal, a process of physical concentration leads to greater consciousness.

The concentration of a conscious universe will reassemble in itself all consciousness as well as that of which we are conscious. The human and the universe are inseparable.

The universal energy must be a thinking energy if it is to be less highly evolved than the ends animated by its action…a transcendent form of personality.'

Members of the faculty, how does a young woman quote this so accurately? Dr. Nazeer, you are comfortable with Zoroastrianism, another of the young lady's quotes? It does provide some basis for Islam, does it not?"

"Dean, certainly, but I'm not comfortable with Madison's understanding of the basics.

Prominent in Zoroastrianism, an ancient religion of Iran which was largely replaced by the Muslim religion, Islam, is a doctrine of the Bridge of the Separator. The pious are helped over the bridge into the House of Song where God dwells forever with his own. The bridge is said to be broad for the righteous but as narrow as a razor for the wicked, where they fall off into hell. The god of Zoroastrianism, Ahura Mazda, promises woe in the House of Druj at the end of existence for the wicked and the House of Song at the end of existence for the righteous.

Zoroastrianism still is practiced in certain areas of Iran and India. Zoroaster, the prophet who lived in the sixth century BCE, wrote the *Avesta*, the basis of Zoroastrianism scripture.

Muslims also believe in the continued existence of the soul after death. Not unlike Zoroastrianism, the Islamic Day of Judgment is described as passing over hell on a narrow bridge, the Siraat, in order to enter paradise. Death in Islam is the termination of worldly life and the beginning of afterlife. It is seen as the separation of the soul from the body."

"Isn't that what Madison said to us?"

"It is, Dean, but she said she knew the House of Song having been there. Go figure. That's what makes me uncomfortable."

"This is going to become an issue for us, I know. How does a young math teacher tell us she has died and then come back while professing to know more than most of us know about theology even with advanced degrees on our resumes?

You do realize that she quoted from His Holiness, the Dalai Lama's *The Universe in a Single Atom*? 'We must distinguish between the operation of the natural law of causality, by which once a certain set of conditions are put into place they will have certain effects, and the Law of Karma, by which an intentional act will reap certain fruits. Even with all these profound scientific theories of the origin of the universe, I am left with questions, serious ones, what existed before the Big Bang? Where did the Big Bang come from? What caused it? Why has our planet evolved to support life? What is the relationship between the cosmos and the beings that have evolved within it? In Buddhism, the universe is seen as infinite and beginning less.'

I think all of you know most of us cannot quote anything like that except for the *Bible*."

"True, Dean, but then she went on with another quote 'From the Buddhist perspective, the idea that there is a single definite beginning is highly problematic. If there were such an absolute beginning, logically speaking, this leaves only two options. One is theism, which proposes that the universe is created by an intelligence that is totally transcendent, and therefore outside the laws of cause and effect. The second option is that the universe came into being from no cause at all. Buddhism rejects both.

Understanding the origin of the universe poses an almost insurmountable challenge. Part of the problem lies in the fact the four known forces of nature, gravity, electromagnetism, weak nuclear force, strong nuclear force are not functioning. They come into play later, when the density and temperature of the initial stage have significantly decreased so that the elementary particles of matter, such as hydrogen and helium, begin to form. The exact beginning of the Big Bang is what is called a singularity. Here, all mathematical equations and laws of physics break down.'

How does one know the Dalai Lama so well that she can accurately quote him? She said she met him, and that's fine. But to quote him exactly is..."

"Has anyone talked with Dr. Pike since her visit? It may be time to bring her into the conversation, as we may be dealing with a brain injury that somehow has accelerated the memory process. As dean, why don't I suggest to Dr. Pike that we meet again? I'll call her.

I apologize for interrupting you, Dr. Nazeer. I just don't like all of this uncertainty."

●

"Dr. Treon, I never have seen you looking so lost. Is everything OK?"

"No, as a matter of fact it is not. Tell me, how does a person so terribly well versed in a subject have to throw in something that is absolute fantasy, especially when we know the person is grounded in mathematics? Recently I met with a former student who graduated with honors, and what she told me is bizarre - simply bizarre. First she told me the following, 'Intelligence existed before matter, for it is outside space-time. It is not local, separate, but yet connected, capable of existing in different states and locations. Our mind can be anywhere, in the human body and out.'

She continued with current theories of the physical world not working and can never be made to work until they fully account for life and consciousness. 'We identify ourselves with our body. Consciousness, however, exists outside the constraints of time and space, which are not physical objects. We created time and space to explain an animal sense of perception.

Death is an illusion in our minds because we identify with our bodies. That means a dead person, while traveling through a tunnel ends up in a similar world. Quantum theory postulates that consciousness moves to another state.' Those are direct quotes from Robert Lanza, MD, Scientist outside Boston, in his work *Biocentrism*. And there is more.

She said there is an existence of life after death, and she is proof. What in the world is next? I don't think I want to invite her back even if she would come back. Oh, towards the close of our conversation which I purposely cut short, she began talking about Hans Peter Durr, the physics PhD who died in 2014. She said she talked with him. Talked with him? She quoted Durr. 'Just as a particle writes all of its information on its wave function, the brain is the tangible floppy disk on which we save our data, and this data is uploaded into the spiritual quantum field. Continuing with this analogy, when we die the body of the physical disk is gone, but our consciousness or the data on the computer, lives on.'

Then she quoted the Dalai Lama. God help me, she did.

'Consciousness lives in a quantum state after death. What we consider the here and now, this world, is just the material level that is comprehensible. The beyond is an infinite reality that is much bigger than that which this world is rooted in. In this way, our lives in this plane of existence are encompassed, surrounded by the afterworld already. The body dies but the spiritual, quantum field continues. No known fundamental force of natural science, gravitation, electromagnetic, nuclear can be detected in the spiritual.

The defining characteristic of mental experience is the lack of a physical sense organ… mental experience…is effectively a sixth faculty in addition to the five senses. I was intrigued when I came to discover that in modern Western philosophy there is no developed notion of a non-sensory mental faculty.'

That last statement truly was from the Dalai Lama, and I think I need a shot of bourbon - a stiff, Kentucky bourbon."

•

"Dr. Pike, what do you make of all of this? For example, Madison told the faculty here at the seminary the following.

'Socrates, 470-399 BCE, known mostly today for the teaching of the Socratic Method, wrote of a near death experience captured in the *Collected Dialogues* by Plato. It may have been a record of Socrates himself having the experience.

She continued to quote, rather profoundly I believe, 'No one knows whether death may not even turnout to be one of the greatest blessings of human beings, and yet people fear it as if they knew for certain it is the greatest evil.'

Then she jumped immediately into this.

'Plato, 427-347 BCE, wrote of a Greek soldier, Er, who had a near death experience following a battle. In his book, *The Republic*, Plato wrote of Er's vision of a light, an immortal soul, reward and punishment, reincarnation and a tunnel.

The purpose of philosophy for Plato was to remember that primal vision of a pure, powerful light. The very purpose of life was to remember that journey between death and birth, to uncover that transcendent vision of light revealed in near death experiences.'

Wonderfully bright girl is she not, huh? She talked to me about Brian McLaren, another theologian and his newer book, *We Make the Road by Walking*. 'So what might we expect to happen when we die? Nobody knows for sure, but...we can expect to experience death as a passage, like birth, the end of one life stage and the beginning of another. Imagine a moment before the Big Bang. Imagine creativity, brilliance, fertility, delight, energy, power, glory, wisdom, wonder, greatness, and goodness sufficient to express itself in what we know as the universe. We can expect to experience as never before the unimaginable light of God's presence.'

She had the faculty stunned."

"Did she talk with you about Rene Descarte, Dean? Listen to what I spoke of with her. She also quotes him.

'Rene Descartes, 1596-1650, writes of Mind/Body Dualism. Dubbed the father of modern western philosophy, he also was a mathematician and scientist. His theory of mind/body dualism is that the nature of the mind is completely different from that of the body, making it possible for each to exist without the other.

The mind is formed of a distinct type of substance not governed by the laws of physics, i.e., substance dualism. The mind and body are composed of different substances, and the mind is a thinking entity that lacks the attributes of physical objects. The mind is a separate entity from one's physical being and lives past the death of the body.

Mental properties involving conscious experience are fundamental properties identified by a completed physics, i.e., property dualism. Mental phenomena are non-physical properties of physical substance. If the human mind is a property of the physical brain, then the mind, consciousness, would end with death of the body.'

She went on to reference William James, 1842-1910, *The Will to Believe*, who wrote: 'The truth is that the present phenomenon of consciousness exists.

Plato to William James: States of insight into depths of truth unplumbed by discursive intellect are illuminations, revelations, full of significance and with authority, all inarticulate though they remain. And, as a rule, they carry a curious sense of authority.'

Jung to James: My thesis then is as follows. In addition to our immediate consciousness there exists a second system of a collective, universal and impersonal nature in all individuals. It is inherited. It consists of pre-existent forms which can only become conscious secondarily. They are culturally shared memes, units for carrying cultural ideas, symbols and practices.'

Where is all this coming from? I simply don't know, and I can't argue the points although I don't know that I would."

"Dr. Pike, maybe we should ask her to come over again. The faculty is interested, and so am I. Of course, we hope you can join her."

"Of course I will. However, I'm not certain where she is right now. She isn't at her apartment in Richfield, her aunt's home over by the airport, or in Cottonwood. I know her mother and Dan are growing concerned."

•

"Rev. Anderson, have you seen or talked with Madison? "

"No. I'm still trying to put my thoughts together before I sit with her again. Here are two examples for you. First, her knowledge of Spinoza is beyond me.

'Benedict (Baruch) Spinoza, 1632-1677, author of *Ethics* was influenced by the Descarte theory that the universe is divided into mind and matter. Spinoza wrote to unify a complete system of the knowledge of God, as his was a rational view of religion, a natural vision, away from traditional religious beliefs.

His book, *Ethics*, attempts to define God's true nature. Spinoza's famous proof that there can be only one substance that is infinite and its own cause consists of two points. First, either nothing exists or else an absolutely infinite substance exists. Second, something exists. Moreover, Spinoza feels only God is absolutely free. Therefore, man does not have independent free will.

God is not the great being many religions make him out to be. In fact, God is substance or that which exists by itself and is conceived by itself. God is both mind and matter.'

What a statement that is, I hope you agree.

Then it was Immanuel Kant about whom she talked fluently even suggesting she had met him or listened to him in person. How, I don't know, and neither does the faculty at Luther. You have dealt with this phenomenon before, Dr. Pike, surely you have some insight. This is what she said about Kant. I wrote it down as fast as I could.

'Immanuel Kant, 1724-1804, wrote that human understanding is the source of the general laws of nature that structure all experience, and human reason gives itself the moral law which is our basis for belief in God, freedom and immortality. Therefore, scientific knowledge, morality and religious beliefs are consistent and secure because they all rest on the same foundation of human autonomy.

What can we know? He asked. Our knowledge is constrained to mathematics and the science of the natural world. It is impossible to extend knowledge to the supersensible realm of metaphysics. The reason that knowledge has these constraints is that the mind plays an active role in constituting the features of experience and limiting the minds access only to the empirical realm of space and time.

The universe had a beginning, a purpose.'

Then Madison told me it does, the universe does have a purpose, she knows for sure having witnessed it.

Dr. Pike that is exactly what she said to me. I wish I knew what this was all about."

•

"Well now everyone, here we sit in Minneapolis without Madison. She is gone, and we have no idea where she is. I have notified the police in the Twin Cities as well as officials in Northfield and Cottonwood. My fear is that she ran into someone who took advantage of her while pretending to be an authority on her experience, but that is highly unlikely.

Dan, thank you for coming. Do you have any thoughts at this point?"

"Dr. Pike, she had so much to do that I'm taken aback by her absence. That simply is not her. No note in her apartment; nothing at her school; no friends have been contacted."

"Sandra Lee, this is especially hard on you, and we know it. Do you know of any place where she would seek refuge from all of this? She did sustain quite a blow to her head when hit by the oncoming car, and she might be thinking she needed to get away."

"No and neither does her father, Roy. She had a few places in Cottonwood where she would go just to read or walk, but they would not be any kind of permanent places. In Minneapolis proper, I have no idea."

"Rev. Anderson, did she say or imply anything to you?"

"I wish that she had. I am just as dumbfounded as you."

"Dean?"

"Dr. Pike, the young woman came to us with a wealth of information some of us knew and some of us have forgotten. She could be a faculty member without question based on her extensive knowledge, so why she disappeared is beyond us."

"I have talked with Dr. Treon at Carleton. He was so impressed with her knowledge of quantum mechanics that he was overwhelmed. He also was not able to handle her near death experience. He repeated a couple of statements made by Madison which may be of importance.

'Waves, energy - quarks and qubits - will seek their original source, if separated from that source, through a wormhole or like entity at the speed of light or faster. The passage through a medium such as a wormhole in space may be instantaneous for the wave, but in earth time, years may pass.

Quarks are elementary particles and a fundamental constituent of matter, waves/wavelets. Quarks combine to produce hadrons, the most stable of which are protons and neutrons, the components of atomic nuclei. A quark has been described as a qubit of information. Three quarks form a qubit. Is consciousness captured in a quark or quarks?'

That is what Madison professes to know for certain.

Meanwhile she said Wolfgang Tittel, PhD, at The University of Calgary transferred a photon seven miles in a quantum state, a wave, by teleportation across a fiber network in 2016. It was done in ten PICO seconds, one trillionth or one millionth of one millionth of a second.

Then she spoke of the speed of light at 186,282 miles per second. A light year is 5.9 trillion miles, and the Hubble telescope has identified an object located in the visible universe that is 5.9 trillion miles long. Madison says she travelled faster than the speed of light and actually saw the object as she passed it.'

Also this, 'Classical physics defines the predictable, deterministic world we see around us. It is the study of matter and motion and the behavior of both through space and time, along with energy and force. Theoretical physics employs mathematical models and abstractions of physical objects to explain natural phenomena.

Quantum physics is the study of sub-atomic particles - quarks, hadrons, electrons, protons, photons. Fundamental particles are not like tiny grains of sand. They are more like waves free to choose from all possible states. If physicists can control the sub-atomic particles, they feel they possibly will have solved the final theory of God.'

Dr. Treon knows that, of course. But Madison, how and why does she?"

"I don't know, and it's frustrating. This whole thing is getting to me, and I am afraid - actually afraid - to see where it is headed. I am a psychiatrist who never has seen anything like this before. Can anyone here address this comment from Madison?

'Mankind continues to study the vastness of space, infinity, timelessness, and the concept of nothingness after death; yet he cannot complete those studies even with superior skill and intellect. True, man has the ability to think, to reason and to rationalize, but that is the limit of his understanding. Equally important is the question, what is consciousness?'

Who can comment on that?"

"I can, but Dr. Pike I don't know that it will lead us anywhere but where we have been. We are dealing with a super intellect of sorts who undoubtedly can take on any subject within any discipline with ease, and a person who is doing it for a specific purpose. Maybe we begin to focus on why rather than what.

"Dean, I can't argue with that at all. Does anyone else have a thought?"

"I'd like to suggest that we view that purpose in only a positive manner. Other than Sandra Lee, I have known Madison since college and know she is a kind and caring person. Whatever her purpose is, it has to be a good one."

"Accepted, Dan. Hopefully all of us remember that and don't begin to suggest she is anything but that. Okay then, I will start the process by going back into her records at the hospital since that's the starting point for all of this."

"Please, Madison is my daughter whose head injury may be behind all of this strange behavior. She is a wonderful girl who may simply be confused right now. Thank you in advance for helping us to find her."

•

"Good morning, Dr. Pike. I'm Mary, Head Nurse on the floor."

"Good morning. Good to see you. Would you kindly pull all of the records for a young lady, Madison, who spent the past few days in room 826? I would appreciate it."

"Dr. Pike, I have been looking through records this morning, and we have none for a patient named Madison. Come to think of it, we haven't had a patient in room 826 for a couple of weeks.

"Check the computer then, would you please? I was with her a number of times in that very room."

"Dr. Pike, I have not seen you on this floor for some time, and this has been my station for a few months. I dare guess I am one of the only nurses who knows you, and that's from my emergency room experience a year or so ago. Let me try to pull up the information on the parent company's computer.

No, nothing although there was a Madison in the emergency room a few days ago. Records indicate she died and was transferred to the county morgue."

"That is correct; she was. I wonder why her records were not updated. Really, this late record updating simply is not acceptable and is going to cause the hospital a problem one day."

"Mary, may I speak with her nurse, John? He was with her in the evening."

"Dr. Pike, we have not had a nurse on this floor by the name of John for all the years I have been here."

•

"Hi, records? This is Dr. Pike in Psychiatry. I'm trying to locate the records for a young woman named Madison who died a few days ago and was transferred to the county morgue. Do you have the updates in the file? It should be easy to find since we haven't had many morgue runs lately."

"Let me check, Dr. Pike. Nope. We have nothing since we discharged her body to the morgue.'

"What about her re-registration when she came back?"

"Came back? I don't understand."

"She was checked back into the hospital after the morgue found she still was alive."

"Go away! How does that happen?"

"Please, just find the records for me."

"I can't. Is there a chance she checked back in or someone checked her in under a different name?"

"Not a chance."

"I buy all of that, but certainly we would have been informed if a discharged corpse would have been checked back into the hospital."

•

"County morgue, this is Dr. Pike, and I'm checking on a patient from Fairview Southdale who was brought to you a couple of days ago. Her name was Madison…"

"Got it right here. It has been very quiet lately and your patient, Madison, was one of our few intakes."

"Good, thank you. I need to know when she was returned to the hospital."

"When she was returned, you say."

"Yes, that was after you or someone there found her alive."

"You got me, Dr. Pike. We never send anyone back, and where did you get that idea? Found her alive, you say? I sure would have known about that."

"Please, I am getting sent from person to person trying to find my patient. Is there someone at the morgue who can find her records?"

"I can direct you to another office, but their records aren't any better than mine. I really don't know that we can help you other than to say she was cremated yesterday since we didn't have any immediate relatives and she was so badly bruised."

"You did what? You cremated her! How in the world, who in the, why in...I need to speak to the Commissioner's Office right now."

"Yes, Ma'am, I'll transfer you immediately."

•

"Yes, I am Dr. Pike from Fairview Southdale calling about a patient who supposedly was cremated yesterday at the morgue."

"Very good, Doctor. It seems we had only two cremations in the past two days, and one was a woman, a Madison…"

"Wait, who gave the order to cremate her?"

"That decision is made by the Commissioner, our pathologist, the Sheriff's office and…"

"That's enough, thank you. May I come over to see the records, and did you take any pictures of the deceased?"

"I'm sure you can, but that needs to be arranged by the commissioner, herself. Did you know the young woman?"

"That's what I'm trying to determine. Thank you very much and please excuse my abruptness for what is becoming a very difficult time for me."

•

"Rev. Anderson, I saw the records and photos of Madison. She died and was cremated according to her wishes which were found in her backpack. The statement of cremation apparently was written by Madison after she died in the car accident, although only you and I would know that. Rev, Anderson, I don't understand. We saw her; we talked with her; we listened to her. I examined her head looking for contusions, scars or damage resulting from the accident. You took her to Luther Seminary. Dr. Treon in Northfield continues to be baffled by the discussion he had with her. Not only that, but I haven't had time to talk with Sandra Lee yet or Dan for that matter. What do you think?"

"I don't know what to think at this point, Dr. Pike, and God knows I have to think about it for a while. If she wasn't here, who was? The dean and the faculty who met with her are going to be shaken to their foundations, that I know and don't blame them. Dr. Pike, I'm not hallucinating am I? This is far out stuff, science fiction stuff."

"Neither of us are hallucinating nor are the professors at the seminary, although they might begin to think so. I owe it to call Dr. Treon at Carleton since he is in the mix of all of this as well. I'll also call Dan. You might be better at talking with Sandra Lee than me."

"What do we say? She died in the accident and never was here. We were imagining all of this. Is it possible Madison was here, that she actually found the light, came back to the same time she died and then went back to the light after leaving a message about the light with all of us. Other than those of us who talked with her, no one else is going to believe this."

"Reverend, I think it's time we began to read about fermions and bosons and quarks and qubits. I think the great minds deserve another look as well be it Kant, de Chardin, Spinoza, Durr, McMillan and Lanza, Rovelli, Hawking and Tononi. No one is going to believe us right now, and I'm afraid we won't believe it either after a period of time. That is a psychiatry textbook fact.

However, I am stuck with the following. Madison quoted Kierkegaard again before she left the last time. 'Life is not a problem to be solved but a reality to be experienced.' Then she quoted Dr. Melvin Morse at the University of Washington regarding near death experiences 'Life is for living, and the light is for later.'

What will the others who met Madison think about that last statement? What do you think, Reverend? Is the light for later?"

PART FOUR

The Conspiracy

THE LAST GREAT ADVENTURE

Part Four
The Conspiracy

"Dr. Pike, is that you?

My God it has been ten years if not more since I saw you last. I'm Dan, Madison's boyfriend - former boyfriend, I should say."

"Well now, Dan, you haven't changed a bit. 'Looking good,' isn't that what Sandra Lee first said when introducing you?"

"Yes it sure is. Your memory is the best, and Sandra Lee's comment was before we had any idea what was about to happen."

"Dan, are you still with Ford in St. Paul?"

"I am, and thank you for remembering that too. I'm in charge of design for our most efficient, self-driving trucks. Can you imagine, today those big engines can roll on down the highway without a driver? Ten years ago, no way would that be a possibility."

"I'm all for it. Having driven in Boston this past summer, I think all vehicles should be self driven. Boston is rated as having the worst drivers in the country."

"Boston?"

"Yes, I did a summer program in psychiatry at Mass General Hospital. Theirs is an excellent program, one of the best in the country."

"Do you ever think of Madison, Dr Pike?"

"I do, of course, and I continue to study quantum mechanics and relativity as we said we all would do so long ago. Maybe I should say I studied conceptual physics without math or the difficult formulas only physics majors would understand. Madison has been a factor in my life every day since I first met her, or first listened to her in the emergency room when she was unconscious, and it still is hard to figure out and accept all that happened."

"Interestingly, Dr. Pike, I was on the St. Olaf campus not that long ago but stayed away from bumping into Dr. Treon. The guy still is shook by all that happened with Madison according to some of the professors I know. Actually they are worried about him and his preoccupation with the metaphysical as well as his use of alcohol. They think he might be working and drinking a little too much."

"No such thing as a little too much. It sounds like he has a problem."

"Dr. Pike, I hate to hurry, but I am on my way to the new sports bar at the Mall of America. You are welcome to join me and meet some of Madison's old college friends. They might give you some new insights into Madison's personality and behavior."

"Very nice offer, but I'm due back at the hospital soon. However, I think it might be a good idea to pull the others together sometime soon. It has been ten years, and that's too much time. I'll check in with Dr. Treon myself as well as Reverend Anderson. Are you up for a call to Sandra Lee?"

"Yes I am, absolutely. We spent a lot of time talking and getting to know each other following Madison's disappearance. She would welcome the call especially since Roy died last year."

"I didn't know that. Is she doing okay?

"She is a complainer as you know, and she thinks she has every ailment known to mankind and then some. Fortunately her boys are close to Cottonwood and have helped her transition to grandmother and matriarch of the family. She loves those roles as you can guess."

"Good. I'll see Rev. Anderson later today and know he will contact the Dean at Luther Seminary. It seems Madison caused a lot of infighting over there."

●

"Dr. Treon, this is Dr. Pike from Fairview Southdale. How are you?"

"Oh, Hello Dr. Pike. I'm fine, just fine if you know what I mean? Been busy, busy as always, and still working on the Madison thing. Speaking of which, have you figured out anything new about her disappearance?

"Dr. Treon, your voice sounds stressed. Is everything okay?"

"Hold on for a second, there we go. You said what?"

"I said that you do not sound good, and from what I understand you may be affecting your role at the college."

"It must be the phone, since I'm not used to my new Bluetooth. Whoops, I dropped the damn thing. Here we go. I'm back on the line. You were saying…"

"Dr. Treon, I suggest you get some rest. You do not sound good."

"No. No. I'm fine. I'm just relaxing a bit here in my chair and can stop drinking or overworking if I decide, and I can do that anytime I want. Hey, I've done it many times over the past ten years."

"Drinking? I can hear it in your voice. You know I didn't say anything about drinking which makes me worry even more. You were most impressive when meeting with all of us in Edina, Dr. Treon, and I'd hate to see you lose your academic edge because you are tired or under the influence."

"Okay, Dr. Pike. I'll keep that in mind. I promise. However, you called me."

"I did, thank you, and just wanted to check in with you since we haven't seen each other for ten years. And no, I haven't made any progress with the Madison case. I'm guessing you have not either."

"You got me, Doctor. Been thinking about it, her, a lot, but still no resolve."

"Okay, Dr. Treon. I'll stay in contact should something surface that is relevant to our experience. Thank you for taking my call and be well. Maybe a vacation is in order? Hello. Hello. Dr. Treon, did you hang up on me?"

•

"Rev. Anderson, I bumped into Madison's old boyfriend, Dan, at the Lincoln Dell today. Do you realize it has been ten years since we lost Madison? Days pass slowly, I'm told; and years pass quickly. Isn't that the truth?"

"So right, Doctor, you are spot on. Good comment especially on top of what I have been saying recently in chapel about faith being a journey and not a destination. I need to deliver a few more homilies to make that theory work for everyone. Oh, don't forget what Madison quoted from Chopra 'Time is the movement of thought past, present and future.'

By the way, how is Dan?"

"Good, he is very good actually. I was thinking it might be good for all of us to get together soon and discuss some of our thoughts over the past few years. Do you remember that I said some of us might doubt what we experienced in regard to Madison? I'm sure that is the case today."

"Well some of the Luther faculty members are suggesting that very thing especially when her thoughts conflicted with accepted religious tenets. That is a pretty conservative group over there, as you know, and sometimes I think they are too far removed from the laity."

"We all get that way, Reverend. Call it fatigue, boredom or laziness, I don't know which it is in their case, but I do know that it is time for us to meet again. Can you help me with that?"

"Of course I can. Let's pick a couple of dates to see if we can make it work."

"Reverend, Dr. Treon will not be joining us. Seems this whole adventure - bad word, huh - has been too much for him. He is consumed with Madison and is overworking himself trying to piece it all together. I'm sure it is his driven and perfectionist ego. I even quoted Ernest Hemingway in *A Farewell to Arms*. 'The world breaks everyone and afterward many are strong at the broken places." I hope he listened."

•

"Sandra Lee, thank you for calling. How are you?"

"Hello, Dr. Pike. It has been a long time, especially for me since Roy passed away."

"I am so sorry, Sandra Lee. I know you and Roy were very close and had been married...how many years?"

"We were married almost fifty years, which seems like a lot of time. He was doing...oh so very well until his heart gave out. Men seem to go out that way, don't they, very sudden and without fanfare."

"I'm not certain that it isn't a bad way to pass, Sandra Lee. He didn't have any pain, and he didn't linger. Long illnesses are difficult on spouses like you who wind up exhausted and sometimes hospitalized when the illness of a loved one carries on and on. How are your children handling Roy's death?"

"Like troopers. They live close by and have been wonderful to me. Plus I take care of the grandchildren all the time which I love."

"That's the best therapy, as you are learning. I'm happy for you on that count.

Sandra Lee, it has been ten years since we last got together and discussed Madison. Would you like to come to Minneapolis to meet with Rev. Anderson and some of the seminary faculty at Luther? I would consider it a personal favor, as I am sure Madison would have."

"Of course I would, Dear. That's what Dan indicated when he called and suggested I call you. Just let me know the date and hour of day, and I'll have one of my sons bring me to the city. I guess we have a lot to discuss."

•

"Madison shared her interpretation of the Machiavellian Intelligence Hypothesis with us ten years ago. 'The ability to reason how cause and effect are related, to understand change and to be insightful, occurred because of the need to manage complex social situations. Once man used language, he could think in words to communicate with himself.'

Profound? Of course. Something all of us understand having studied Machiavelli? Certainly. Something a woman who professed to dying and returning to life said? You bet. Someone who told us consciousness does not die? Again, yes. But why? Why did she do it? And why did she then leave? As Dean of the school, I still do not have the answers.

Dr. Pike, I once again thank you for pulling all of us together here at the seminary. I believe you told us we would doubt the events with Madison ever occurred, and you were correct. Personally I do not doubt my sanity, but I do question my understanding of the meaning of the experience. Your earlier comments led me to recognize Madison as a source of intelligence well beyond my, our capacity to understand. Could she have been a master of disguise with an IQ well above 200? That surely would account for her ability to leave us questioning each other."

"Dr. Pike, I'm Dr. Nazeer here at the seminary as you recall. Thank you again for calling this meeting. Is it possible we are dealing with a form of alexithymia? Madison was brilliant in regard to her understanding of theology, philosophy and science. But she talked to us with an obvious lack of words for her feelings. As you know, that's alexithymia. How could she have gone through all that she professed to have gone through with a lack of feeling for it? She almost was cold. I questioned her sincerity and honesty due to her superior attitude."

"Whoa! Those are tough questions. She certainly had feelings when I talked with her, but her amnesia and trauma may have affected how you heard her or how she projected herself. Good question, Dr. Nazeer. I have to work on that."

"One of Madison's statements caught me off guard, Dr. Pike, and those statements still ring true to me. That being the Stephen Hawking view of an atomic explosion versus the Big Bang. According to Madison, Hawking said 'An atomic explosion does not create life. The Big Bang would if there is an intelligent creator.' I absolutely love the statements, as they reinforce our position that a creator, a supreme lawmaker is behind all of this. I do not know if Hawking is an atheist, agnostic or believer in God; but the statement itself leads me to believe we could talk with him. I am getting away from our purpose in being here today, but it all relates to our experience with Madison."

"Thanks for the comments, Dr. Nazeer. I honestly do not know that I remember hearing it from Madison. However, everything she said and did have to add up to the reason she was here. Where ever she is, if she is anywhere, she is ten years older today unless she went back to...I don't want to consider where she might have gone back to. The fact that we have no records of her being here or with any of us has no relevance. We saw her; we talked with her; we were close to her. Surely one of us has an explanation after having considered this for ten long years."

"Dr. Pike, thank you again for inviting me. Early on I spent time worrying that one of you here today took advantage of my daughter and imprisoned her somehow. Her wealth of knowledge concerning matters we don't understand suggests even the government might want control of the situation. I've read there is a lot of that going on in the world."

"Sandra Lee, that is preposterous. You are talking to educated people of high morals and ethical standings who would never even consider such a thing. As Dean of the faculty, I would like to close that thought, that possibility immediately. And concerning the government, they didn't even know of Madison's so-called adventure."

"That's unless she went to the government, Dean. She had a number of appointments scheduled, and who knows, one of them might have been with a government influential. The morning she left me in her apartment, she was on a mission even though she didn't tell me or leave me a note as to where she was heading. Doesn't our government work in secret most of the time? What other entity could erase all records of her leaving the mortuary, returning to the hospital and staying in room 686? Sandra Lee, I haven't even thought of the government's involvement in the past ten years. With all the science fiction movies about aliens being captured and studied, however, maybe you have hit on something.

Hey everyone, if she told anyone in the government that she knew about the James Web Telescope tuned to observe the early universe and black holes or the

Event Horizon Telescope photographing the shadow of a black hole on surrounding light, they might have arrested her as a spy."

"Dan, you are into conspiracy theory. I suggest we go very slowly here."

"I suppose you are right, Dr. Pike. Do you ever read or listen to our St. Paul neighbor, Garrison Keillor? He once wrote or said 'If you learn nothing else from great literature, at least you learn that the nicest people are capable of the darkest deeds.' Madison and I used to read Keillor for fun and listen to his radio show in college. We never ever considered his statement to be a factor in our lives especially in Northfield, the town of colleges and cows or something like that. But now, today, I am wondering."

"I am looking at the faculty nod with each other. The possibility that the government jumped into this is too much for all of us."

"Dean, I side with you, but we came here for a purpose. Maybe we had best chase down this theory mainly because it is the only one we have?"

"I agree, Dr. Pike, and I volunteer to lead the search. I work with the government on a daily basis at Ford trying to stay within the Fed's automotive guidelines. They are tough if not impossible types who are not warm and friendly and who could do most anything, much to our chagrin."

"This discussion has gone on a tangent I don't think any of us expected. Are there any other thoughts, even academic thoughts that were questioned ten years ago but are proven now?"

"Dr. Pike, only in the area of quantum mechanics have there been advancements we can associate directly with Madison, and I don't know that any of us can speak to that discipline. Maybe one of us should make an attempt to talk with Dr. Treon in person? I'd take on that role since the seminary and St. Olaf are related by Church ties, although my preference would be to find more of the Dead Sea Scrolls in Qumran. If only Madison had told us something like that, then we would have no question about her journey, her so-called adventure."

"That is a wonderful initiative, Dean. Thank you. Are there any other comments? It would seem to me that any of us having a command of a subject just proven true in quantum mechanics such as waves or wavelets holding our consciousness, would add to our credibility if, and it is a big if, we ever decided to go public with our experience. However, that is a subject for another time."

•

"Dr. Treon, it's great to see you again."

"Dean, likewise. I trust your drive down to Northfield was enjoyable. The weather sure is wonderful this time of year, and the Ole students are ready to forgo afternoon study to catch some of that warm sun we finally are experiencing. I'm guessing you remember those days."

"I do, certainly. You know, Dr. Treon, I see God in nature, and watching the fields turn green with the creeks running high is nature at her best. Not only that, but there were more than a few young calves and ponies visible from the highway. Nice time of the year is correct.

Have you ever read Deepak Chopra? His *Seven Spiritual Laws of Success* includes these great statements. 'The universe is movement of energy and information. We are a part of it. Nature is a symphony.' I love that.

However, I'm here because I have a question for you that relates to our experience with Madison ten years ago. Have there been any significant findings in physics or cosmology that relates directly to all or anything Madison shared with us? I think you know what I am referring to, something that was discovered after she left."

"I know. I have wracked my mind and hurt myself health wise trying to find something that would prove her experience with us. She said she saw new technology and new leaders of the world. Trouble is she didn't say exactly what or who other than it was, and I have wasted more than a few hours simply trying to remember."

"What about Einstein's theory of the static universe which was new to me ten years ago?"

"Nothing new there. Theoretical calculations in 1917 showed the static universe as modeled by Einstein was unstable and contradicts general relativity. The theory stated the universe was expanding due to the continuous creation of matter. We now know the universe is expanding due to dark energy which is seventy percent of the universe, but we still do not know what it is or where it comes from. Madison said she witnessed the universe beginning to expand again five billion years ago, but that already had been found by research. Interestingly, Einstein was of the opinion our galaxy was the universe. In 1925 Edwin Hubble proved the universe included more than just our galaxy and in 1929 that the universe was expanding. He proved the expanding universe was finite in space and time. Try grabbing a hold of that theory, huh? Then on February 11, 2016 scientists announced they had detected gravitational waves confirming the final part of Einstein's theory of relativity."

"And the Hubble telescope…"

"The Hubble satellite is no bigger than a school bus, although back then putting it 380 miles above earth in 1990 wasn't something done every day. Today the Hubble mirror estimates there are over 2 trillion galaxies in our universe alone. Hubble continues to move at 17 thousand miles per hour, is billions of times more sensitive than our naked eye and sits above the distortion of the earth's atmosphere. Now there is talk of putting another telescope, mirror outside the moons orbit. Can't imagine what that will show us.

Don't forget Madison also talked about the new James Webb Telescope and the Event Horizon Telescope."

"You are over my head. What about consciousness?"

"Not much there either. Think of it this way, a salmon egg hatches in the far regions of the Kenai River. The salmon then runs down the Kenai and into the ocean swimming in circles for two years while eventually finding its way back up the Kenai to spawn. How does it do that? We say nature or instinct whereas it could be cellular memory, plain and simple. Proving it is another matter. Madison didn't do that for us even though she acknowledged cellular memory. Too many of us call it muscle memory when it could be wave/wavelet memory."

"Energetic cardiology?"

"Good one. It has been proven, but like a transistor, it remains mysterious. We only know a transistor affects another physical system and what happens to that physical system. Confusing? More simply stated, we only know how a physical system affects another physical system – not why."

"Fermions, bosons?"

Already found. But the question remains, do they hold consciousness? We don't know. Madison said yes, but we can't prove it and we don't even know how to try. The world would kill for that information if Madison had it.

CERN, by the way, continues to look for and isolate a particle smaller than a quark. I'm all for the project, as you can imagine, but I think they should be attempting to communicate with a quark rather than just find isolate parts of it. Is that a bit too much? Of course it is, and has been for too long."

"Nothing is too much these days it seems. The electromagnetic field?"

"Nope. Nothing new there either. It carries radio waves, fills space, vibrates, oscillates like the surface of a lake, and transports electrical force. It remains stronger than gravity but acts only on charged particles like waves. Sounds like Madison talking, huh?"

"Multiple universes?"

"You have to talk with Hawking or Rovelli about that."

"The origin of energy?"

"All we can do is measure energy. We can't account for it. It's kind of like trying to identify God, and exactly like trying to account for dark energy."

"That's my line, Dr. Treon. Some of us think we have identified God. By the way, you are a wonderful resource. Thank you."

"No, thank you, and please extend my thanks to Dr. Pike as well. This whole mess with Madison coming and going has put me to the wall as noticed by Dr. Pike. I have been working and drinking much too much for ten years but have just slowed down working so hard and have quit drinking. I even have help with my family holding me on a tight rein. You know the power of family, Dean. I believe in family and maybe a 'higher power' at work in me as well"

"I have a few more questions beginning with the ESA."

"Interesting observation. The European Space Agency is on a five year mission to map and measure the Milky Way. They are looking at the makeup, position, motion and characteristics of a billion stars. Madison, if she had been there, surely could have added some data to the study. But she didn't leave it with us."

"How about the Hawking theory of a multiverse?"

"Gotta send you back to Hawking and Rovelli again. All I can do is ask myself just how the universe is expanding, where is it going? That, in and of itself, adds credence to the possibility of multiverses. What else is out there? I'd like to think God has the answer and that we will someday. Maybe Madison had or has the answer? Maybe it's the quantum fluctuation theory she supported?"

"Mars?"

"Madison said it flips. Actually she said she saw it flip. She was correct in that Mars flips every 120 thousand years as proven by the ice caps becoming the planet's equator. Madison also said it wobbles which it does. Earth does neither due to the gravitational force of the moon. What Madison said and what we know are proven correct. If she also is proving it to us, wonderful, but I can't take that to the bank now that she is gone."

"Jupiter?"

"I love Jupiter. Why not? It is 5 years away at 165,000 mph which totals 1.8 billion miles. Almost too much to comprehend for a non-scientist, it has a mass of one-thousandth of the sun but 2 ½ times that of all the other planets in the solar system. Not only that, but 1000 earths could fit inside Jupiter. That's 1000!

Madison said she saw the Juno spacecraft about 3,100 miles above the surface sending radio signals to earth that took 48 minutes to reach us. Madison was correct, of course, she always was. But once again, I can't take that to the bank."

"Black holes?"

"It may be that what we know as black holes are responsible for the formation of galaxies. Madison said that, and sure enough it is being proven true. She even said the bigger the black hole, the bigger the galaxy. Black holes grow by accretion taking in gas and space dust as well as planets and stars over millions of years. We also have found merging black holes.

Think of the Milky Way, Dean, it is spiral, as you know. That's due to the push of dark energy and the pull of dark matter. The center is 26,000 light year from earth, and that's where we find a black hole. And please don't forget, Madison said she saw another black hole in our galaxy.

It's interesting to know we'll never get out of our galaxy since it has billions of stars, is 100,000 light years across, 100 light years thick and holds our tiny solar system within which is our tiny planet, earth. Almost too much to accept, don't you think?

Now I have a question or two for you, Dean."

"Absolutely, Dr. Treon, go for it please."

"The 'thin place' about which Madison talked, what is it, a hologram?"

"Madison referred to the 'thin place' when talking about the Transfiguration on Mt. Hermon and then again when Mary saw Jesus at his tomb. Jesus said 'Do not embrace me' to Mary, since he was in a space between what we call heaven - for lack of better words - and what is earth. In other words he wasn't approachable in a physical way. The same happened later when Jesus, Moses and Isaiah were on Mt. Hermon, if one believes that event took place. It makes sense for a number of reasons, one of which is that Jesus hadn't fully come back - neither had Moses and Isaiah. In those days two witnesses had to confirm an event like that which the people saw. Isaiah and Moses were the witnesses. With regards to Mary, were witnesses necessary? Maybe not? Believe her or not.

So let's take this a step further with Madison. She certainly wasn't in a 'thin place' especially with her relationships with her mother, Dr. Pike or Dan. Why? I don't know. The 'thin place' surely would have thrown all of us if she approached us that way. Then again we all would be deemed nuts if we began saying she was here but not here. I don't know that any of us have experienced the thin place or thin space."

"What about her thoughts regarding consciousness?"

"Now you have me trying to recall her words. Madison kept coming back to thinking, feeling, intuition and sensation, the Myer-Briggs indicators. She also talked about synchronicity, meaningful coincidences. Think about something; talk about something; then it happens. Are we seeing into the future, she suggested? I believe she was trying to help us understand all of that."

"How about the evolution of mankind? You and I know man became self-aware when adapting to his environment. Nature adapted and resonated with the environment as well. But then she said something else that I can't quite remember."

"I do. She said man became self-aware and less impulsive."

"Right. I missed that last word, impulsive, and it is so straight forward.

Finally what about your church's stand on heaven or hell?"

"Remember Ian Barbour and his comment regarding taking the *Bible* seriously but not taking it literally? Well, look at the *Old Testament.* There is no doctrine of heaven or hell found there, so that pretty much tells us what we need to know. That plus the old three tiered universe isn't seen as it used to be.

Don't forget, the *Old Testament* had a focus on salvation, specifically salvation from the Roman occupation, especially since Judaism does not have a doctrine of afterlife."

"Dean. This has been more than educational for me, and I suggest we do it again. Thank you."

"No, the thanks go to you, William. We will for sure, and I'll keep you posted. Good luck with learning to relax more. You are a better man for it."

•

"Morning, Dan."

"Morning, Mr. Diedrich. How's our bulbous government doing today?"

"Still there; still growing; still more regulations. There has to be a better way, although don't threaten my job, please."

"Got ya! By the way, do you know anything about the Veterans Hospital over by the airport and the security wing, speaking of growing? I drive by it a lot."

"I know that we have some top-secret stuff going on there, but that's about it. Somehow or other a leak got out last month suggesting some major breakthrough in quantum mechanics had occurred. You and I have talked about wave theories with subatomic particles, but the excitement over there suggests more than anything about which we talked. Who knows, maybe it's a major breakthrough taking place right here in Minneapolis St. Paul."

"Interesting. Quantum mechanics, huh? Why there? Oh well, I have the specs you need for the new self-driving tanks. We can make them here or turn them over to your facility in Lima, Ohio. I'll be interested in how the bidding goes."

"I want the tanks made here, absolutely. How else can I preserve my job in St. Paul? Plus I do not want to move to Ohio anytime soon with my kids so solidly in place in school here. They are right across the river at Minnehaha Academy, love it and can walk to school on a nice day. Can't beat that!"

"Speaking of quantum mechanics, who is in charge over there? I'd love to get some ideas for our work here, since anything new is bound to be an advantage for Ford. Look at it this way, any new information we have dealing with qubits will help keep you in St. Paul."

"I really don't know who runs the ship over there, but I'll see what I can find out. You have my attention, Dan, as long as it isn't industrial espionage."

"Ha! We're not sophisticated enough for that stuff, Diedrich. Plus I don't want to go to jail, ever. I'm too young and pretty."

•

"Please wait in your car, Sir. Who wants to know about the VA Hospital?"

"Me, Diedrich! I am a Fed employee, you know, and I don't appreciate such a curt response. Not only that, but I do have rank over you. Check my badge again, please."

"Sir, I am required to ask the question. I don't like it anymore than you, but orders are orders. The Veterans Hospital has changed significantly over the past ten years. It's something about finding a breakthrough in science."

"Understood, thank you. My daughter is thinking of doing some volunteer work over there, and I told her I would get some information first. Does that clear me, or do I need to go through a metal detector?"

"Okay, I got it. The woman in charge of administration is named Ackerman. She is a former college administrator and has been in St. Paul for a long time. I have met her, and find her to be very nice considering the senior role she plays in that old building. The security couldn't be tighter in the research wing, and I'm sure the pressure is noticeable. Why? I don't know since nothing has been announced to this date about a scientific breakthrough."

"Thank you. I'm sure my daughter won't be near the security wing if she does the 16 year old candy striper thing."

•

"Yes, I do have credentials to enter the hospital, most any hospital for that matter. And yes, I know the chief administrator, Em Ackerman. We have attended a couple of educational seminars together, and she is one of the best in her field. The hospital is lucky to have her. You probably don't know that she turned down the offer of CEO there? Family and environmental issues were her reasons. Smart lady.

But Dan, just because some top secret research is being conducted there doesn't mean it involves our Madison. Plus the idea that she might be held there against her will is balderdash, since I know a person like Em wouldn't allow it."

"I don't know, Dr. Pike. Maybe she doesn't know anything about Madison, and the CEO does. We are dealing with the government remember, and they are capable of doing anything? History tells us that, no?"

"Dan, I have to think about this for a while before I call Em. A cup of coffee or lunch certainly is possible, but approaching her about a secret study on quantum mechanics might not be on the menu. I remember laughing with her about the UFO conspiracy and the JFK hidden files. I also know she loves the Star Trek movies, but the Madison thing may be a bit too much for her or anyone."

"Okay. I'll continue to do some digging here, but let me know what you decide, please."

"Of course, Dan"

•

"Dean, it is a pleasure meeting with you. I worked on education committees with former administrators in Minneapolis who attended Luther. They couldn't speak highly enough about the seminary. However, how do I wind up having lunch with a seminary dean and my friend, Kay Pike, who comes from a totally different discipline?"

"Ms. Ackerman, let me tell you a story that you will find hard to accept - if not impossible to accept. It happened ten years ago and has ramifications today."

•

"Ms. Ackerman, I have no idea what you are talking about. Research at this facility has to be oriented to medicine otherwise we lose funding. You know that, Em. Then your talk of a separate wing housing quantum mechanics research far and above what is happening at the university or corporate level - not to mention the government - surely can't be accepted as anything but speculation and hearsay. Don't you think that as CEO, I am informed of everything happening here?"

"Ronald, over the past ten years we took in over eight million dollars for quantum research. What is that all about? Our chief financial officer can't account for it, and she put it on the balance sheet as miscellaneous medical research. Huh? I checked further and found the IRS didn't even question it. Really, eight million dollars! Maybe that's a pittance for the government, but it sure isn't for us. As Chief Administrative Officer, I'm surprised we haven't been audited personally for the missing, miscellaneous monies."

"Ms. Ackerman, you are going where you shouldn't be going. I'd simply let it go and concentrate on the administration of what we know for sure. Just questioning the missing eight million will bring in everyone from the press to the Department of Veterans Affairs to senators and representatives. It could cost us our jobs."

"Ronald, what if, just what if it cost a young woman her freedom? You tell me, what's worse than that - to be a prisoner in America for nothing illegal? You tell me, what's worse than snuffing out a person's life? You tell me…"

"Her life has not been snuffed out nor is she a prisoner!"

"What? What did you say, Ronald? Come back with that statement again, what did you say?"

"I said the conversation is over, and you had best forget it. People will kill for the information we have developed. I am most serious, Ms. Ackerman, people will die if this gets out."

"If what gets out, Sir? What could possibly be life or death information coming from an old and tired veterans administration hospital?"

"Thank you, Ms. Ackerman. Time's up!"

•

"Hi. I'm at a loss as far as what to tell you. From a business perspective, I have found nothing but a huge, unaudited amount of money. From a personal and ethical perspective, we have a real problem, Kay. Fortunately, I'm not concerned about losing my job but I may lose it as soon as you and I get involved in the secrecy at the hospital. And we are going to get involved in a major way."

"I don't understand."

"Let's meet for lunch tomorrow with the dean. We are going to have to pull in some political heavyweights to get to the bottom of what I am going to tell you."

"I'll check with the dean regarding lunch, Em, probably somewhere close to the university. It's a halfway point for all of us."

"And preferably a loud place since we don't need to be heard. I feel threatened already but can't say for certain. Maybe it's just nerves, I don't know, but I do have that sick feeling in my stomach."

•

"Good evening, and thank you for tuning into WCCO radio - the source for all your news in the Twin Cities. A traffic alert is just in from I 35W and the Crosstown Highway where a multiple car accident has taken the life of the chief administrator of the Veterans Memorial Hospital here in the Twin Cities. Details are forthcoming, but the accident appears suspicious to the police as an automobile slammed broadside into the car in which the Veterans Hospital executive was killed instantly. The driver of the car in question immediately ran from the scene leaving what we have learned is a stolen car. At present, the police have no idea why the driver purposely rammed the deceased's car. We'll follow the story throughout the day."

"In Duluth this morning, the Vice President of the United............"

•

"I'm sick, Dan. What have we done? Em Ackerman and I were to have lunch today along with the dean of the seminary. She called me yesterday suggesting we meet in a loud environment in order not to be heard. She also suggested we call in some political heavyweights, and that she was getting nervous. I'm not used to this kind of drama at all especially when it involves murder, if that's what it is."

"Let's get Dr. Treon back in on this, as he sounds like he is back on track. It probably will be a relief to him knowing he wasn't going crazy. Plus his thoughts may prove valuable."

"Dan, one more thing, let's not use a phone for any conversations. I am going to call Sandra Lee to inform her that the government isn't involved, and we'll have to look elsewhere for answers. If anyone is listening, hopefully that will appease them. Now I'm sounding spooked, don't you think?"

"We all may be soon, Dr. Pike. I'll drive down to Northfield and see Treon. Meanwhile meeting here at the Lincoln Dell probably is a good spot for us."

•

"Dr. Nazeer, what was the demonic Legion's exact number?

"6826 and the Devil's, 666. Hasn't Hollywood played up those numbers over the years?"

"Yes, but what room was Madison's at Fairview Southdale?"

"I believe 826, at least that's what Dr. Pike, Dan and Sandra Lee said."

"On what floor?"

"Dean, I know where you are going with this. It's a bit of a stretch, don't you think?"

"I don't know what to think at this point. Room 826 on the sixth floor – 6826, Legion. My God, if the room had been 666, I'd be a basket case."

"You are looking too hard, Dean. Don't get yourself tied up like Dr. Treon."

"At the time of Christ, a Roman legion consisted of 6000 men plus 700 or more horsemen along with enough others to total 6826. Why do we find ourselves talking about Legion and the number 6826?"

"Because you are tired, Dean, because you are so very tired."

"I suppose. I'm having a meeting with Dr. Pike, Dr. Treon and the young man, Dan, this week. Please join us."

"I'm Happy to. Where and when?"

"I'll let you know.

•

"First things first. I suggest we table this conversation for a few weeks just to make certain no one catches onto our discovery - if that's what it is, a discovery."

"Yes, a deadly discovery at that, Kay. First Madison is gone and now, Em Ackerman."

"Em Ackerman, isn't she the woman who was killed a few days ago. You know, the chief administrator at the Veterans Hospital."

"It's more than that, Dr. Treon, and may I call you William?"

"William, please."

"Dan explained a lot to you when he was on campus, but he purposely left out the murder of Em Ackerman until now. The police have no idea why the driver of a stolen automobile rammed Em on the highway. We do, of course, but we don't know what to do with the information."

"If secret research on quantum mechanics is happening at the Vet's Hospital, that's enough for murder if it is breakthrough stuff. I mean, you are talking about time travel, fusion bombs, multiverses, scaled up quantum superposition…"

"Hold on William, please. Why fusion bombs? That isn't new is it?"

"It is if we can control fermions and bosons, subatomic particles. Governments, corporations, you name it would kill for that control. Maybe someone already has?"

"My God, I think I am going to be sick. Dear, dear Em, what did I get her into?"

"Not your fault, Kay. This would have happened sometime to someone sooner or later. Keeping information of that type under wraps forever is impossible. You found out by accident. Some of us at Olaf might have found out by accident, who knows? The question is what do we do with the information now? I don't think holding off for a few weeks does any good. Whoever did this to Ms. Ackerman surely has sights set on finding out who else knew.

Dan, did you say you talked with a person at the Fed by the name of Diedrich?"

"I did. He often works with us making certain we conform to government regs."

"Diedrich was found dead this morning outside the Fed office building. Seems he had a massive heart attack. He had St. Olaf connections which is why I found the announcement on my iPhone app. Okay folks, it's time to get some outside help. I don't believe in coincidences, and this isn't a coincidence by any means."

"Dr. Nazeer joined me today to serve as a sounding board among other things. Do you have any thoughts, Dr. Nazeer?"

"Dean, before my family left Pakistan, we had many, many dealings with the government. It was terrible. Family members were taken away; property was confiscated; and money became the only means for survival. How else does a man like Bin Laden get away with hiding in the country for so long? Money! Life itself came down to one thing - and that was money.

It isn't all that different here, as you know. If what you say is true, then a life changing discovery in the field of quantum mechanics is valuable beyond your dreams. Any entity, government or corporate, will stop at nothing - absolutely nothing - in order to control it. Look at the furry caused by the first atomic bomb as an example.

I agree with Dr. Treon. Let's get some outside help now. Whoever is behind the murders of Ackerman and Diedrich will not stop until all threats are eliminated. You know only too well that the worst qualities of mankind manifest themselves when money is involved."

"I hate to say it, but it's time to go back to work. Thank you for joining us for coffee everyone. I will get back with each of you soon, so save your thoughts for a time when we can talk privately without fear of wiretapping or intruders. You can catch me most any time at the hospital or on my cell."

•

"Senator, it is wonderful to see you. Thank you for finding time in your schedule."

"Kay, stop it. You know you can come see me anytime, anytime at all here in Minneapolis or Washington. What you did for my husband and his depression is something neither of us will forget - ever."

"Chronic traumatic encephalopathy, CTE, is becoming more and more of a concern. I feel badly for all those who suffered from it years ago but couldn't be diagnosed. Hopefully all medical doctors will go looking for it rather than wait for symptoms after there is a major head injury on file."

"Kay, I know you wouldn't come see me unless something serious is going on."

"Yes, I believe I know who killed Em Ackerman and a fed employee by the name of Diedrich."

"Kay, Diedrich was my cousin on my mother's side. Our whole family is shocked. He was an honest, hard working family man that lived for his kids and friends. Why he would be killed is beyond any of us. We think - thought - it was a massive heart attack."

"Senator, this is going to get dicey. Let me brief you on what I know."

"Hold on. Sally, please hold my calls. Thank you."

•

"Good morning, Twin Cities! You are tuned to WCCO TV - your news source for politics, sports, weather, local news and the arts. Speaking of which, the Twins won Thursday night in a blowout. We'll cover that win in Tampa in a minute along with a forecast of some very warm and sunny weather coming in.

Also last night, WCCO News Action Alert was informed the Veterans Administration Hospital was secured by the Federal Government RICO Division.

A top secret research wing was found to be in violation of government spending and record keeping as well as being implicated in two murders, one of which was the automobile ramming of the former chief administrator of the hospital just last week on the Crosstown Highway. The second murder was the cover up of a federal employee who was said to have died from a massive heart attack outside the fed offices. Coroner's records appear to have been compromised, and the death now is said to have been caused by lethal injection.

We are told - on the record - top secret, scientific information was being developed at the hospital while diverting funds intended for use with patients and staff. The story will be featured throughout the day and of course, tonight."

"Yes, Dr. Pike, you have clearance to enter. The individuals with whom you would like to talk are in conference room six, and they are expecting you. As you know the former chief administrator was killed, and the CEO has been removed from his position and is under house arrest. Too much is going on these days for this old facility."

"Gentlemen, I am here for one reason only, and that is to determine the whereabouts of a young teacher, Madison…"

"She is not here, Dr. Pike. The woman came to us ten years ago with a far out story none of us could accept until she left a formula for separating a quark into fermions and bosons. We have been working on that formula ever since she left. As a matter of fact our former CEO had designs of making us all rich once we confirmed the formula worked. He personally killed a Fed employee, John Diedrich, in the Fed's parking lot by injecting a lethal drug, and then convinced the coroner Diedrich died of a heart attack. The CEO had the right credentials since he is an M.D.

He also brought in 3M on a consulting basis in order to determine what they thought of his - not the young woman's - idea. 3M, Medtronic, Cray all consulted with no success. After ten years of intense work, we are convinced her theory, formula, will work, but we are missing one element. We can't find the source of energy for the waves. It's an enigma."

"Back to Madison, please. Where is she?"

"We have no idea, and believe me we have looked for her. I know your offices were scoured trying to get a lead on her whereabouts. Cottonwood and Northfield locations were searched by employees of our CEO, and Dan's apartment was searched. Oh yes, we knew about Dan. We even hacked the records at the hospital thinking we could cover up most anything, and we could have if there were any. The records were gone. I am afraid the lure of millions corrupted us all, and now I think we are looking at major problems."

"You are looking at major problems, Sir, but that is not mine to determine. When Madison left, did she say where she might be going?"

"No, and we didn't care at that point. The CEO was so taken with the idea of capturing the market in quantum mechanics that he became a different person. However, one thing still bothers him. How did Madison write a letter instructing the mortuary to cremate her? I know he spent a lot of money - government millions - buying off people after she disappeared, but he still didn't get an answer regarding the letter. It looks like he'll never get the answer now."

"Who killed Ms. Ackerman?"

"A local felon contracted by the CEO. The police have him in custody and know him from his past arrests. Damn, we didn't know the CEO's actions would take this course."

•

"Thank you all for coming over to the hospital. First, I did not tell any of the personnel at the Vets Hospital what we think happened to Madison. That would open a whole new topic that we don't want them aware of mainly because we can't trust them. That includes the CEO, of course, who is on his way to prison. I remain sorry for Em Ackerman, although she would have become involved somehow, someway. The missing eight million dollars, the secured wing of the hospital, the IRS - she would have found out and become involved. I'm certain the CEO wouldn't have let anyone jeopardize his opportunity for fame and fortune at that point.

Second, we are back to ground zero in our search for Madison. I'd like to think we will see her again, but after ten years and all that we just discovered, I doubt we will. My preference is I hope, really hope, she went back to the 'light'.

Dean, Dr. Nazeer, Dan, Reverend Anderson, Sandra Lee, I'm at a loss once again, as I was ten years ago, but I honestly believe she is alive and is in a safe place - somewhere out there peacefully with the 'Lawmaker' or the source of energy itself. But once again, as it was ten years ago, all I have is something she left for us before she disappeared, something Einstein wrote.

'A calm and modest life brings more happiness than the pursuit of success combined with constant restlessness.'

I don't think any of us can disagree with that, at all."

PART FIVE

Incident at Northfield

THE LAST GREAT ADVENTURE

Part 5
Incident at Northfield

"Excuse me, Sir; do you know what that was?"

"Not a clue, friend, although I have to guess it was a meteor or one of the 2,600 or so old satellites that no longer work. We'll probably see a ton of them streak through the sky sooner or later. What did I see on cable recently? There are over 170 million pieces of space junk up there with almost 30 thousand pieces of some size, all traveling at 17,500 mph."

"Amazing numbers. However, with North Korea rattling swords, light streaking across the sky concerns me."

"No way. It was too small and didn't have an aftershock. Plus we wouldn't be here talking if it were a North Korean atomic bomb. Not only that but it was moving much too fast for anything I've ever seen - anything man made, that is. It is strange though, I was sure I could see the beginning of the light and the general vicinity of the landing site all at the same time. It looked like it came from outer space and not just our outer atmosphere."

"Yeah, almost like an outer space lightning bolt, although what else could move that fast?"

"Nothing I know of."

"The speed of light is what…around 186,000 miles per hour?"

"Yeah, something close to that, although nothing can move faster than light."

"I don't know about that. Doesn't quantum mechanics deal with waves or wavelets, you know, subatomic particles that can move faster than the speed of light?"

"Huh? Quantum what? You lost me, friend."

"Sorry. I like science fiction, and quantum mechanics is a popular theme for the writers. Seeing that light makes me think of sci-fi stuff."

"I suppose. We'll read about it tomorrow. I can see the headlines now, friend. 'Streaking light baffles scientists; origin and landing site can't be confirmed; our government doesn't know what it was.' Your sci-fi people will love it."

"Yes sir, they will won't they. And to think, we saw this today up close and personal. Never had a chance to say that before. Oh well, have a nice day."

•

"This is KSTP Radio reporting in Northfield, 45 miles south of downtown Minneapolis St. Paul. This morning a white light ascended to earth and touched down in a large cornfield just west of the St. Olaf College campus. However, authorities were not able to find an impact site, damage or any sign of debris.

St. Olaf Physicist, Dr. William Treon, visited the site immediately after impact and said the light touched ground almost as gently as a rainbow. 'Faculty and students witnessed it, somehow sensed an impact when it touched down, and swear it moved with so much speed they could see the origin of the light as well as the touchdown at the same time. Presently we have detectors on the ground determining if an unknown entity - if there was one - was radioactive, although there is no sign of radioactivity at this time.'

Students sunning on the hills west of campus on what the college calls Hoyme Beach, ran for cover not knowing what had happened. They also indicated there was a wave of air, almost like a force field, that moved through them without putting anyone off balance. One student said her watch stopped; another, her iPhone needed to be rebooted. One stunned student reported, 'I felt something - a wave, maybe - move right through me. It was like I was floating in the ocean and drifting on a swell.'

Seems strange things are happening in this college town of Northfield, Minnesota, sometimes known as the town of 'Cows, Colleges, and Contentment.'

This bulletin just came in to the station. The physicist at St. Olaf who was first on the site, indicates a small, very small burn mark was found at the site of impact. 'At this time we have no idea what caused the burn mark which appears to be no wider than that of a pen or pencil. We would not have found it if not for the witnesses indicating exactly where the impact took place. Finding it is a miracle of sorts, although the burn mark penetrated wood, corn stalks and an old metal wheel leaving a marked trail before touching down. Now our question is how deep an impact was made, if at all? Interestingly if the burn mark is real and that small, whatever landed here must have been much smaller.'

Off the record, Dr. Treon said 'If Shoeless Joe Jackson of the White Sox walks out of the cornfield ready to play baseball on the Field of Dreams, it will be time for me to retire.' KSTP will stay on this story throughout the day."

•

"Dan, our clocks are off by...one second according to the calibrations. Any idea what caused that?"

"I didn't notice but the robotics did, and I don't like the hesitations on the production line. It may have been only a second, but the jarring effect made me uneasy."

"Even if the power shut down, which it didn't, the clocks wouldn't have slowed and the robotics wouldn't have been affected. I wonder what's going on?"

"Weird. Really weird."

"Hold on, there's an important announcement from headquarters on the Big Brother screen."

"This is Ford Motors in Detroit with an important announcement from senior management. We have concluded a cosmic shock wave hit the earth today causing an almost unnoticed effect other than resetting all clocks and timing devices back one second, including those in Ford facilities. The multiplier effect of that adjustment has been felt on most everything at Ford from our robotics, systems and programs to our satellites. The most dramatic effect on satellites has been the adjustment of our cesium atomic clocks. The cesium atom is a metal that is liquid at room temperature and oscillates, cycles, at 9.192.631.4.770 per second. All of you who are physicists know that means we are addressing a serious problem in space right now. Hopefully, the effect on Ford plants worldwide will be minimal. We will keep you informed of future developments. Thank you."

"When they talk cesium, Dan, aren't they talking quantum mechanics, one of your favorite subjects?"

"Favorite, yes, but cesium is not quantum. It's a chemical element, and no way can I fix the satellites, Driscoll."

"Remember the problem they were having at the Veterans Hospital? Wasn't that about quantum mechanics?"

"Don't remind me, Tom, Minneapolis St. Paul still hasn't figured that one out, although they know the former CEO is in prison for life. You know the score, RICO problems, premeditated murder and the biggest, his ego. The guy turned out to be a ruthless killer - all for money."

"Did Ford ever get into discussions with that CEO as did 3M, Cray and someone else?"

"Thank God, no, because one of us might have gone the way of Diedrich. Remember?

Tom, what does the one second mean for our robotics?"

"Danny Boy, big trouble if we don't get it reset fast enough."

•

"Dr. Pike, the intranet went down as did the whole backup system. Other than that, everything seems to be normal. The printout of your patient's heartbeat seems to be off by a fraction, maybe not even that. It has to be the equipment and not the patient."

"Any word from the administration? If not, then we keep working as normal. Funny, even my cell phone had a glitch. This kind of problem can't happen in a hospital like Fairview Southdale, so someone had better be on it. Do you remember a few years ago we lost records for a patient? It drove me nuts trying to piece that together, so hopefully this isn't more of the same."

"Dr. Pike, check this out on our hospital cable."

"This morning a bright light streaked through the northern sky and appeared to land south of the Twin Cities. We have on-site reports from station KSTP reporting from Northfield as well as from people on the ground.

At the same time, power disturbances were felt across the world specifically as it relates to time. Meteorologists here at WCCO tell us a second disappeared on clocks everywhere on the planet. Why? We don't know and probably would not have noticed. We are told, however, the President's National Security Advisor is in touch with all countries capable of causing such an outage. Russia, China and India already have expressed concern about the disruption and are working with our government. Some are saying this is the very effect we expected at the turn of the century when we adjusted clocks and computers from 1999 to 2000. This time the ripple effect on clocks alone could be disastrous.

Presently government authorities are descending on Northfield as we make this broadcast. The entry location of the light is the primary focus. St. Olaf Physics Professor Dr. William Treon is on-site and will talk with WCCO shortly.

Stay tuned. This has all the elements of a major event."

"St. Olaf is in the news again along with William Treon. He's a pretty good choice for the college to oversee this."

"You know Dr. Treon, Dr. Pike?"

"I do. We have much in common going back to the horrible events at the Veterans Hospital including the murder of my friend, Em Ackerman. He was more than helpful resolving that situation for the police and for me. Nice guy.

What comes around goes around, don't you think?"

"Is he married?"

"Please, I have no idea. I do know that he an overachiever, perfectionist and one heck of an instructor. I'll have to catch up with him sometime to find out what is happening with the events in Northfield, since I'm sure he will get totally involved. Meanwhile we need to make certain our systems don't malfunction again."

●

"Thank you for joining us this morning for our weekly chapel service at Fairview Southdale Hospital. I am Rev. Anderson, as many of you know.

I have changed the subject of my homily this morning due to a very interesting development in Northfield. We have learned a white light travelling at an amazing speed struck close to the city and its two colleges, Carleton and St. Olaf. Thought by many to be an alien probe from another planet or another UFO sighting – and a serious one at that - government agencies have been put on major alert while the President of the United States has done the same with the military.

Meanwhile our Governor has suggested we curtail any travel south of Burnsville on Interstate 35W unless absolutely necessary. She also has activated the Minnesota National Guard.

Is this an overreaction? I certainly think so even though our clocks and intranet malfunctioned briefly. Now I'm told the internet was affected as well. If what has happened is a sign of life on another planet, then maybe we should welcome it rather than take a defensive posture. If it is an attack on our infrastructure by a hostile force like terrorism, then we must defend ourselves!

Don't forget St. Augustine and the just war concept as is written in *The City of God*. Evil is out there, and good and bad things happen to the righteous as well as the wicked. It's warfare between the God and the devil. Our friend, Augustine of Hippo in the Fourth Century, wrote *The City of God* in a response to Christianity bringing about the fall of Rome. His foe, although different in name from ours, still is the same. It is evil named Beelzebub. That name is in *Luke*, Chapter 1.

Now, before some of you jump on me for delivering an old time fire and brimstone type homily, remember we do not know what is happening in Northfield. We will shortly, to be sure. The key here is to address the solution - the right solution. All we have to do is hold tight until the excitement settles down and we have a reasonable explanation, which could be as simple as cosmic radiation. Personally, I hope so for all of us.

I trust everyone feels a prayer is appropriate at this time."

•

"William, any idea how fast that light really was traveling?"

"Faster than a lightning bolt, Professor. It's a simple deduction since lightning bolts can be seen from cloud to ground and travel pretty close to the speed of light. This light was seen in space or coming from space while being on the ground all at once. How high it was, I don't know, but surely it was better than the fifty or sixty miles to the border of space and probably much higher than 380 miles where Hubble sits. Don't forget GPS satellites are 12,400 miles up; and communications satellites, 22,000 miles up. None of them picked up the effect of the light other than adjustments of time. I'd venture to guess it came from outside our galaxy at a speed much faster than a picosecond.

NASA's Chandra X-ray observatory launched in 1999 didn't pick it up either. That surprises me since it applies microlensing to coordinate the gravitational signature of planets orbiting extremely distant stars. Why it found a planet outside our galaxy 3.8 billion light years away - the first time that ever has been done - but didn't pick up the light that just entered earth, I don't know.

By the way, I got caught up in picosecond measurement better than ten years ago."

"What for, William, another set of graduate orals?"

"No Professor, the situation involved a missing woman, a teacher who graduated from Olaf and lived in Richfield. She had what we determined was a near death experience, but it was unlike any near death experience we had heard about before. She indicated she traveled faster that a picosecond, faster than one trillionth of a second to and from earth, and had the ability to prove it."

"Is that what took so much energy from you during that time?"

"You bet. You philosophy profs have it easy philosophizing all day. Only kidding, of course, but I got lost trying to answer the whereabouts of the source of energy of which she spoke, drank a bit too much trying to settle my nerves down, and almost lost focus on what is important, like my family."

"Been there. I became a friend of Bill's, AA, and learned a lot. I'll tell you William, there are so many things out there that can get to us. I found the beginning of drinking usually marks the end of intimacy. That comment is straight out of an AA book, *Relationships in Recovery*. Fortunately I read that and reacted before my marriage was shot and I came close to ruining things, let me tell you."

"Thanks for sharing that. So far I have pulled out of the potential tailspin and feel great. Plus this strange happening in the cornfield has me excited, and I hope we find something. Maybe we'll celebrate over a soda one day off campus, especially if the universe just dropped us a breakthrough in quantum physics."

"William, I almost forgot with all the excitement. You said you knew something about the recent announcement concerning the Dead Sea Scroll fragments. That's why I came over to your lab."

"I did, yes. The sixty tiny fragments detailed the festivals that marked the end of the seasons from the Second Century BCE to the First Century CE. Ten years ago the young woman from Richfield about whom we just talked, knew that.

She said she saw them in one piece and when stored in the caves at Qumran. I was blown away last week when I read the report. And you wonder why I admit I drank so hard these past ten years."

"William, someone told you about this before it happened? I don't understand at all."

"Professor, neither do I. We'll have to get together later and discuss this."

•

"Dr. Treon, the impact of the light entering the ground is dramatic, and we don't have the technology right now to determine the extent of penetration. This thing, as I call it, probably went deeper than the earth's crust. If it were as small as you say, there may not be an effect on the earth's surface, but still we don't have any idea what it is. I have no idea what effect it would have on the earth's core - if it made it that far down."

"Captain Cusick, let's contact NASA and find out where muon technology is being used to penetrate rock. You may remember muon technology recently found passageways inside pyramids previously thought impenetrable. If anything can locate whatever this is, muon technology is our best choice."

"Now that I think of it, one factor we need to consider is the planting of an alien device that could multiply itself or even disturb the earth's core. The National Guard is enclosing the area around the entry point and may enclose the area around the entire cornfield."

"And Shoeless Joe will appear."

"I'm sorry, Sir. I didn't get that."

"Oh, one of the college's cows, Shoeless Joe, is out there wandering someplace, Captain."

"I see, Sir. We'll look for her."

•

"Dr. Treon, the colonel says we will have the muon technology tomorrow morning thanks to the Air Force. It will arrive in Minneapolis tonight and be flown by helicopter here before dawn."

"Thanks, Captain. That's great. Let's get some rest and hope the evening doesn't bring us any surprises. Let's hope this is a good thing or nothing at all."

•

"Good evening, Minneapolis St. Paul. This is WCCO News.

Incident at Northfield, as we now are calling it, will apply new, muon technology - quantum technology - tomorrow at the site of impact in Rice County. Our staff science director will explain quantum technology in a special report at seven tonight. Meanwhile the Air Force is flying in equipment to conduct the search in the area of impact. The Minnesota National Guard has cordoned off the entire cornfield outside Northfield as they begin searching for any signs of disturbance in the area. Reporters from around the world are beginning to descend on Northfield and deliberately are being kept away from the campuses of Carleton College and St. Olaf in order to protect the schools' privacy.

Well viewers, this is turning out to be a very interesting event.

Twins are in Tampa again tonight taking on the Rays…"

•

"Boys, did you hear the announcement from WCCO?"

"What announcement, Mom? The only thing I heard was a light touched down, or something like that, west of Northfield."

"Boys, the physicist in charge at St. Olaf is the same, Dr. William Treon, I met when trying to locate Madison. He once said he didn't believe in coincidences, and I believe what is happening there is not a coincidence."

"Sandra Lee, let's no go there again. Madison is gone; the whole thing is crazy; and it has been years since her accident. I don't want the kids to get excited or confused if we begin to talk about Madison again."

"You keep your ears open everyone. I know about these things. Maybe Madison is coming home after all, and maybe that light is the light she referred to when with me?"

"Now Mom, all of us are together, so let's enjoy dinner as a family, especially with the grandkids. Northfield also is a bit of a drive from Cottonwood, so don't plan on going there too soon.

Kids, pass the veggies and bread, please, and maybe the decanter of chardonnay for your grandmother."

•

"Early this morning police escorted NASA's muon technological equipment from the Air Force hangers at the Twin Cities airport to Northfield. That equipment is being set up as we make this broadcast and is being supervised by a civilian, Dr William Treon, a physicist at St. Olaf College. WCCO will stay on site and will brief you on progress. We also learned drilling platforms are being installed around the corners of the field and impact area but do not know why at the time of this broadcast.

Dr. Treon! Dr. Treon! WCCO here. Do you have a minute to talk?"

"I do, certainly. Muon technology or quantum technology as it is known, will give us an indication of what kind of impact the light made on the crust of the earth. More important, however, is the final settling location of the light. If it changed direction or bounced off limestone sediment or water, both of which are prevalent here, we have no idea where the light finally came to rest. God only knows if it exited the earth."

"Dr. Treon, do you feel we are looking for an alien entry point?"

"I have no idea and can't imagine aliens here in Minnesota. Plus I don't want to speculate so early in our research. What I do know is the speed of light was surpassed by this entity or wave, whatever it is. I'm estimating the wave of light, if you will, travelled at gigalight year speed. That's over one billion times the speed of light, the speed of light being 5.9 trillion miles a year if you remember your high school physics. Tough to digest that speed, huh? If the object moved that fast, then it would go back in time. We need to find out if that is why our clocks were set back a second. Certainly the light may have been travelling that fast; but why did our clocks turn back? We'll find out, although to date, science has never measured anything that fast."

•

"Members of the Physics Departments, please excuse my formal address. We have entered a period of unusual activity here at the college. As soon as the muon equipment is ready, we'll be in the cornfield looking for answers for which we will have many questions, I'm sure.

One, however, will be most difficult. Why did clocks around the world lose a second? Have we witnessed a reversal in the 'arrow of time?' Have we witnessed a glimpse of a mirror universe where time moves backwards? Did the light come from a wormhole confirming an assumption of theoretical physics that time travel is possible? Worse than all of that, is the possibility that we have experienced a time warp. Would just one second affect anything? Absolutely! That we will find out very soon and not comfortably, I'm afraid.

If Ian Barbour were here, I'm sure he would have something to say. Would anyone from Carleton like to jump in at this point? Mr. Chairman, what do you make of all of this?"

Thanks, Dr. Treon. At first I thought it was gravitational lensing with the light being warped by the solar system itself. Then I began thinking about gravitational cones in a black hole pulling time and space together. Finally I thought about miniature wormholes, although short lived and impossible to measure. However, your comment about Shoeless Joe coming out of the cornfield took me back to reality. I thank you for that.

Truth is I don't have an answer, but what I find myself dealing with is the n-body problem of predicting the individual motions of a group of celestial objects interacting with each other gravitationally. Was this thing, this light, cast off by a group of celestial bodies ridding themselves of an unnatural force? If so, we have a new theory to apply to the n-problem.

Or was this the effect of two black holes forming a wormhole that connected the earth and the black hole? How's that for far out thinking?

Think about what Margaret J. Wheatley wrote in *Leadership and the New Science*. 'Quantum theory introduces yet another level of paradox into our search for order.' Even though she was dealing with the corporate environment and not just science alone, she knew what happens. 'At the quantum level we observe a world where change happens in jumps beyond our powers of prediction.' Well folks the light certainly made a major jump, and presently is beyond our powers of prediction."

"Could the FRB 121102 signals to earth of 15 bright light radio pulses from a dwarf galaxy 3 billion light years away have anything to do with this? I ask that because our department here at Olaf has been studying them for the government. So far the fast radio bursts study hasn't proven conclusive."

"William, I don't know, but it's another avenue to pursue. We'll send you our findings re FRBs from the Carleton Labs to see if they help.

Your favorite statement regarding no such thing as a coincidence may have play here. Why the light? Why the cornfield? Why here in Minnesota?"

"Let's talk wormholes. My first actual experience with wormholes was a number of years ago. Trouble is I couldn't and still can't prove it, but we know labs have created an invisible tunnel, a magnetic field through space. That said, we know that tunnel might be the size of a pinprick. Question arises being, how do you measure the pinprick which may last less than a second? If so, could this light have been a tunnel, a pinprick, through space carrying information with it? Our department here at Olaf is going to approach the research with that as our focus."

"Agreed. Great idea. Why doesn't our department at Carleton focus on photon, quantum teleportation? China successfully teleported a photon from earth to a satellite in space, 311 miles away. Maybe this is what's going on with the beam of light from space?"

"Excellent everyone. We are making great progress with whatever has landed in our lap. Thanks for coming over to the St. Olaf campus."

•

"Dean, it has been a while, but do you remember Madison specifically describing the Dead Sea Scrolls with us?"

"I do, Dr. Nazeer, but there wasn't any substance to it until now. We had some idea about the content of those shards, but of course, not to the extent of Madison. Had we acted on her testimony, we would have been able to prove she actually experienced death and returned. I have to believe it is too late now."

"I don't know about that. I took notes and dated them when she visited with us. If those notes can be proven to have been written ten, twelve years ago, then we have something."

"Go for it, Dr. Nazeer. If you are up to reopening the Madison Case, I'll support you. Maybe we should contact Kay Pike and William Treon?"

"Speaking of William Treon, he is all over the news today. The beam of light that struck just outside of Northfield is under his supervision with agreement from the military. Big assignment for him."

"Dr. Nazeer. I haven't checked the news for days while trying to wrap up final grades with the registrar. What beam, what light?"

"Dean, please sit down. This is going to take a few minutes."

•

"Sir, the results are astonishing. The light leveled out shortly after it hit the ground - no more than a foot beneath the surface. Then it ran sideways towards your campus before descending again, fully penetrating the earth's crust and stopping - or being absorbed - when it hit the earth's core. You need to walk with me a few yards in the direction of the campus and check out what we found."

"Really? You actually found something, Captain Cusick? I honestly didn't think we could."

"Oh, we found something alright. Look over here. The light apparently widened to the width of a…let's say small cylinder, is the best way to describe it. And the imprint sits about 5-6" deep. Then you'll see the path of the light going straight down again.

My limited scientific background suggests something was deposited, but I don't know yet."

"Who else knows about this?"

"The senior officer, Colonel Munyon, knows since it is government equipment. How Washington will describe it, however, is another subject. The drilling rig personnel are away from the conversation and may well be packing up soon. We are safe from speculation there, but if the military decides to go looking for something, look out Northfield. Town privacy will be gone."

"Somehow we have to prevent that from happening. Do you know where the officer in charge is working?"

"Colonel Munyon's tent is on the side of the cornfield, or what's left of the cornfield. I couldn't believe how fast they stripped it, Dr. Treon. Maybe we should build a baseball field here for your cow, Shoeless Joe, wherever she is?"

"You've got that one right, Captain."

•

"Dr. Treon, we will be taking over from this point on. I'm sure you understand. If something was deposited here, we have to find it be it drugs, espionage material, unclassified maps or cash to support terrorism."

"Colonel Munyon, what leads you to assume contraband or other material was deposited or flown in?"

"Drug cartels have been firing rocket-like missiles - contraband - over both our southern and northern borders for a year. We don't know what propelled this light, as you call it, but footprints around the area you just examined tell us the contraband was tracked closely and picked up quickly. I expect we will clear out soon and let things get back to normal around here. Quite a scare, don't you think?"

"Quite a scare, yes. Do you have any government physicists on site, Colonel? Our government and others raised alarms when the light first appeared."

"No, Sir. We pretty much know what is happening, although we have to be prepared for anything. That's why so many descended on this cornfield so fast. Can you imagine if it had been something from outer space? This whole county, Rice County is it, would have been turned into an Area 51.

The cosmic shock wave we felt came at the same time the light appeared. Some coincidence, huh? I don't know how that set clocks back a second, but I suspect you physicists will beat that issue to death."

"Some coincidence, yes, but I honestly don't want to think about something coming from outer space? No one is prepared for that around here or anywhere for that matter.

Colonel Munyon, who will be studying the direction of the light and the depth of the light's penetration into earth? Hasn't some of that been recorded already by NASA's technology?"

"Case closed, Dr. Treon. Right now we have to find the people responsible for sending contraband into the country. I'm sure the government's physicists would be happy to hear from you, but getting money to do more here is damn near impossible"

●

"Dean, thank you for coming down to Northfield. It has been crazy around here, and I never could have made it up to St. Paul. How have you been?"

"William, I am just fine, except for the traffic due to the goings-on here. Really, it's a bit too much. But I finally am here, and I continue to miss the conversations we had a while back."

"We'll do it again after this incident, without a doubt."

"William, I wanted to talk in person about Dr. Nazeer having kept her notes when Madison was with us. Madison told us about the Dead Sea Scroll shards that were just translated and released to the public. She told us what they were, the contents of those shards - all of them, 11 years ago. I know you remember all of that. Most importantly, Dr. Nazeer is having her notes officially dated in order to give us some credibility if we ever go further with this. It's almost too much to accept."

"Dean, I can't believe it. As you know, I have told people here about Madison's revelation. We don't have any choice if it proves, absolutely proves, Madison knew that back then. No one can ignore the truth."

"I knew you'd say that. Until then, what do you suggest we do?"

"Let's get in touch with Kay Pike. Her input will help us understand how the public will react. We are talking serious stuff here that could do more harm than good.

Let's try coincidences as well. You are aware of the light that touched down in one of the adjoining cornfields?"

"Another reason I am in Northfield albeit the number of cars on the secondary roads almost kept me from getting here."

"Well it has nothing to do about caves like the ones in Qumran, although we have a cave on campus that Jesse James used when hiding out after the great Northfield raid.

Dean, something is not right. The light everyone saw was not the result of a drug cartel sending contraband in a missile into the U.S. as the government reports. I also don't believe clocks loss of one second was the result of a cosmic shock wave alone. Meanwhile a person close to the site of the impact couldn't have missed seeing a package or container, and footprints at the site do not mean the light was monitored closely and picked up, especially when so many students were viewing the event. The truth is the government doesn't have a clue and is treating this too lightly - if not ignoring it altogether. I plainly do not know why unless they don't want to spook the world while knowing full well what happened and consequently are keeping it under wraps."

"Your take then?"

"Dean, we are back to knowing nothing as we were when Madison disappeared, but this time it's thanks to the government. Dean, something is telling me there is a connection here. I almost can feel it."

"Maybe so, Gentlemen. Maybe so."

●

"Madison? What..."

"Gentlemen, you are looking at a likeness to a hologram. I know you understand the 'thin place' having discussed it some time ago regarding Mary Magdalene meeting Christ at his tomb when He said 'Do not embrace me.' This is the only way I can project myself since my earth body, matter, is gone. The nice thing about that is I don't need it. Neither will you one day. However, in this case, you truly cannot embrace me."

"Then you were the light or in the light."

"Yes, of course. I was in the light and decided this would be the logical place to return especially in view of the conversations you two have had. The drama of a light streaking across the sky originating from the other side of a black hole and touching ground at the same time was necessary. Wormholes are not as small as science hypothesizes, and shock waves accompany the wormhole since so much in space is being displaced so fast.

Dr. Treon, you know the mathematics of that, as wormholes have been created in the lab although very short lived, tiny and not measurable. Dean, you know the principles of that having spent so much time with William.

Wormholes are real, and Einstein had it correct when theorizing the folding of time and space. The only way for me to come back is through a wormhole."

"Hold on please. You said you decided, Madison? You have the power to make the decision where to go and then follow through?"

"It is much easier than that Dean. We decide. Yes, we decide both as a unified entity and as an individual entity. That is what it's like on the other side of the light. We decide as one with a power unlike anything known in this universe.

Think of it as balance, if you will. Lao Tzu understood balance when he wrote *Tao Te Ching* in the fourth century. Balance is the Way or the Path - the Tao. The Way has existed before the creation of the universe; it was created from nothing. We sometimes laugh about the Yin and the Yang terminology, but Lao Tzu was correct using it as a symbol of balance. Maybe I should simplify that by saying life and light.

Pierre Teilhard de Chardin also was correct when he said 'The universal energy must be a thinking energy...a transcendent form of personality.' You remember the Noosphere about which we talked - the collective unconsciousness of humanity? De Chardin knew each individual facet of consciousness would remain conscious of itself in the end. His also said 'The human and the universe are inseparable.'

I am the manifestation of all of that. I am a representation of de Chardin's Omega Point, the supreme consciousness."

"And the black hole, Madison?"

"Dr. Treon, your universe exists in a black hole along with its two trillion galaxies. As a matter of fact, many universes reside in black holes. We can talk about that later. Right now I want you to be comfortable that I am back and am truly here even if in the form of hologram - the thin place."

"As long as you are not a fabrication of Star Wars, Madison, I am comfortable, but I also have so much to ask you theologically. First, where is God in all of this?"

"First things first, Dean. I will use the term God with you rather than another. The word God, however, is too simple to define what is in the light. The name God or Yahweh or Allah or Brahma or Jehovah or Yeshua or Great Spirit or whatever was given the name of a supreme entity by man as he tried to identify that which he couldn't understand, doesn't approach the true entity. Until you enter the light, you will not understand. As a result, I cannot describe God to you as you would like. Please accept that statement.

With that said Dean, remember what Spinoza said. 'God is nature, infinite, necessary and deterministic.' God is everywhere, Dean, in us, through us, around us. Yes, God is energy, the creator, the sustainer, the deliverer. All of us carry God with us, although some not so well as others. God is not just out there somewhere. He truly is in us. He is our conscious, and we must listen to Him.

You also have to listen to Rabbi Kushner, Gentlemen? 'We are living in the continuous presence of the divine.' God, the lawmaker, the source of energy isn't simply 'up there.' God is as much a part of us as we are of God, one within each other."

"Madison, why did you leave ten, eleven years ago?"

"Man doesn't have the capacity to absorb too much too fast, Dean. Look at the difficulty the faculty had at the seminary with my presence. Look at how difficult it is for your parishes to hold onto values and traditions passed down from generation to generation. God's intent, God's will, is to let you know enough while still being part of, what was my favorite term, 'project humanity.' Your neighbor at Carleton, Dr. Barbour, said it clearly. 'God's actions in the world can be thought of as the communication of information, from DNA to computer networks.' Limited communication aids our understanding of how God thinks right up until we enter the light."

"Please go back to the black hole, Madison."

"William, all black holes retain the memory of everything taken in. Stephen Hawking theorized the outer rim of a black hole holds a record of everything the black hole absorbed. It does. It also holds much of what it has taken intact. That's why I said the universe as you know it remains in a black hole. Don't skip over the fact that both the outer and inner event horizons are the focal points of no-return from anything entering a black hole.

Gentlemen, what I am about to say will take all of your creative and analytical ability to accept. I came from a massive galaxy, M87, an elliptical galaxy that can be seen from earth. It was formed by the merger of two galaxies and sits 53 thousand light years away in Virgo. The heart of the galaxy is a black hole the equivalent of three and one half billion of our - your - suns. I traveled from another universe that exists in that massive black hole.

My journey to the light took me out of your universe to M87 and into the black hole. The Hawking string theory and the Rovelli loop quantum gravity theory of multiple galaxies applies here. Your capacity to absorb this is limited, although Julian Huxley had it right, 'We are evolving to a new kind of existence.' Huxley called it Transhumanism, our destiny. He knew we were evolving to a new kind of existence that will understand all there is."

"Are you telling me there is such a thing as a mirror universe?"
"Yes and no. You are thinking too far ahead of me, William. We are evolving yes, but not to a mirror universe; and I am not from a mirror universe.

William, science has been working on reversing the dynamics of the movement of heat to cold. You may be involved with that at the college. What if movement from cold to heat occurred spontaneously? That would reverse the arrow of time and create the mirror universe. Is it possible? Absolutely!"

"Singularities, Madison."

"That reality has been proven correctly, William. The point at which the space-time curvature becomes infinite is in a big bang or big crunch - the singularity. It is when there is no return from being taken into the black hole, and everything is concentrated. Rovelli and Hawking have written much about this, and it was John Wheeler who coined the term, black hole, in 1967 even though the first one wasn't discovered until 1971.

Hawking radiation is the only thing emitted from black holes. Electromagnetic radiation such as light, cannot escape from a black hole. I don't mean to be talking down to you, but I do want to reinforce your understanding."

"What about Phi, Madison? How correct was DaVinci?"

"1.618 is the fundamental building block in nature. Plants, animals, human beings possess dimensional properties that adhere to the ratio of Phi to 1. DaVinci called it the Divine Proportion, and he determined it without the aid of a computer. Think about that, and then think about that in the universe. Everything is related, as we have discussed.

Divide the number of female bees by the number of males in a hive, and you always get the same answer, 1.618 - more females. Also the ratio of each spiral's diameter in a mollusk nautilus always is 1.618. The theory is well known, but the intellectual capacity to discover it was amazing at the time of DaVinci."

"Madison, I need to enquire about theology. *Genesis* once was called The *Book of the Creation of the Beginning of the World."*

"Dean, you remember all the books of the Pentateuch were not named originally including *Genesis,* the book of the creation of the world - the beginning. The first words of the book or theme of the book was sufficient. *Exodus* is a good example and an easy one. An exodus from where? From Egypt, taken from the word Mitzrayim meaning an imprisoned place, a tight spot. That gives a reader of the book a whole new outlook on what happened."

"Madison, what are you? Yes, you appear as a hologram to us. You refer to it as the thin place about which we have talked. You have no substance, no mass, nothing really."

"Gentlemen, you are getting it. I am a wave or wavelet as you like to call it. Think of me as pure consciousness captured in a quark, three fermions. Think of me as three quarks compromising a qubit. That is the easiest way to explain what I am."

"What about Jesus?"

"Dean, you recognize Jesus as having had more effect on mankind than anyone before or after, and He gave us the truest, most wonderful messages ever. The 14th Dalai Lama feels Jesus traveled to Tibet, Kashmir and India learning from Hindu and Buddhist religions only to bring back the best of all of them for us. Jesus was a man; he was a prophet; he now is with God, the Lawmaker, the source of energy, the Creator of all of us. Don't forget that Mohammed was a prophet as well known as the Seal of the Prophecy. Jesus knew the way, the Tao, if you will."

"Madison, you skirted the question."

"No, Dean, there are so many opinions about who Jesus was and who Jesus is that you have to decide while here. I can't do it for you. Just know Jesus is the same as God, the light, the source of energy as we all are when we enter the light. John Hick, *Evil and the Love of God*, wrote 'Christ is the new Adam.' Christ was the new Adam, and we are a part of that. Did Christ have the same ability to return from the light as I have, as others? What do you think happened at the transfiguration on Mt. Hermon with Jesus, Moses and Elijah? Isn't this becoming clearer? How else could the three have presented themselves if it were not similar to me in a hologram-like, 'thin place' appearance?"

"I don't know what to think right now. The *Book of Life*, Madison, what about the *Book of Life*?"

"*Philippians* and *Revelations* tell us everyone's name is in the book. What the book does not tell you is that everyone has moved on...on to the light. The writers of the books did not know that."

"Are we truly the chosen people?"

"Dean, the word chosen has so many meanings, but the *Bible* says nothing of chosen people other than, if prophets were chosen for the Israelites, then the people of Israel were chosen. If they were the only chosen people, who would be not chosen? Why would there even be a people not chosen? What happens to them?"

"What about the covenant God had with His people?"

"There were only four covenants, as you know. The first was God revealing himself to Moses on Mt. Sinai; the second, the ten plagues set upon the Pharaoh. The third took place at the parting of the Red Sea; and the fourth again at Mt.Sinai with the Israelites entering the Promised Land. Let me ask you, do you think God intervened with any other nations? Actually, do you think God intervenes at all? We can talk about that later, but those events in the *Old Testament* are the justification for the covenant Israelites have with God. They also provide the basis for being called a chosen people."

"Madison, back to Spinoza, please. What did he know that others, including us, not know?"

"Spinoza knew God was substance, or that which exists by itself and is conceived by itself. God is both mind and matter. Isn't that very easy for me to say, especially after my adventure having been to the light? Of course, I did not understand it before. How could I have?

John Locke's 17th Century Essay *Concerning Human Understanding* captures the sequence of the growth of understanding very well. Put yourself in the same position today. At birth your mind is a blank tablet. Then a combination of sensations and reflections, feelings and perceptions, forces you to think. As a result of thinking, complex ideas are formed. You are more than developing complex ideas right now when discussing all of this and seeing my image.

Think about John Hick who wrote that humanity was created as immature and is maturing.

Remember Descarte? 'I think, therefore I am.' He was addressing a different subject, but it relates to ours."

"Madison, I should not ask this question, but I need to. What about microgravity and space travel for mankind?"

"You aren't going to have to worry about it for a long time, William. In space there is gravity, of course, but it is microgravity as you know which reduces bone matter in addition to making us lighter. Extended periods of time in space already have had negative effects on astronauts such a losing bone density and lengthening of the spine which can be dramatic. The exercise routine required to maintain normalcy in space is arduous and is going to be a problem for extended travel. By the way, it already is a problem."

"Madison you came and a cosmic shock wave hit us. What…"

"Dr. Treon, the second lost in time already has been adjusted. The effect of my travel to and from M87 more than one time formed a time warp which can't be accounted for with your measurements. The scientists and others working on the one second lost probably are shaking their heads right now. They are asking, how was the lost second was replaced? Why are we now functioning normally?"

"Madison, the faculty at the seminary may ask me if you are an angel."

"Of course I am but not in the sense that you expect. There have been many before me, although we are not sent. We come when we feel it is necessary. Many Catholics firmly believe in Guardian Angels, while Thomas Aquinas defined all of us in *Summa Theologica*. Please take notice that we come in many forms, not just angels. Coincidences, flashbacks, ESP, senses, feelings, perceptions - holograms - all could be one of us communicating with you. Don't get lost looking for wings, feathers and white robes. The movie, Michael, did a great job in bringing the lofty angel back in focus on earth.

Now you know more than most, Gentlemen, but less than all. Importantly God gave us free will. What good would 'project humanity' be if we were robots?"

"Madison, I have to call my office and tell them I'm not coming back today."

"No, Dean, go back now. I have others to whom I need be of service. We'll talk again very soon."

•

"William, she is gone, just like that!"

"So am I gone, Dean; I'm in shock. We are going to need a lot of time ourselves to manage all of this, and we'll need to do it together so that we remember. The *Bible* required two witnesses for certain events, and you and I are the two witnesses in this, the 21st Century. Already I wonder how many others out there have had this kind of experience."

"William, we need to write down questions. What about Noetics? What about Orwell's comments? What about Victor Frankl and people the likes of Hitler, Stalin, even Pablo Escobar? I have hundreds if not thousands of questions."

●

"Mother, Sandra Lee, its Madison. You knew I was coming didn't you? Mother's intuition."

"Madison, I talk to your father all the time even though he doesn't reciprocate. Someday I will approach the light as you did, and then Roy and I will communicate again. Yes, I believed you would come, Dear. I told the boys."

"You will communicate with him again, Mother, for sure. The time it takes to get to the light is instantaneous, although years might pass for someone left behind and not on the way to the light. So think of it this way, Sandra Lee, if Roy's trip was instantaneous as yours will be, you'll be there at the same time even though years pass on earth. You see, time has no bearing away from earth."

"Once again you are talking over my head, but I think I understand some of it now. Wait until I tell the boys. Oh, just you wait until I tell the minister."

"No Mother. You cannot. They will not accept it and will be concerned you are slipping mentally, like they did years ago after the heart incident. When I leave, let it go. The time for you to join us will be soon enough. Promise?"

●

"Dr. Nazeer, how nice to hear from you. I trust all is well."

"It is Kay. Thank you for taking my call. I have some information that will interest you. The Dean presently is in Northfield meeting with William Treon discussing the same matter.

A recent announcement concerning the Dead Sea Scrolls caught our attention at the seminary. It's not that the information is life changing immediately, but it is information Madison gave us eleven years ago. I wrote it down and dated it at the time. If we can ascertain the dating of the note, we will have a means to prove that someone, Madison, was here with us. The Dean and William are determining the plausibility of convincing the public of that."

"How forward looking of you to take the notes, and so very smart! I am sure Dr. Treon is encouraging the Dean to go for it if the dating is reliable. Dr. Nazeer, this could be a major breakthrough - life changing. Amazing! Excuse me for a second. There is someone at my office door."

"Hello. Please come in. I'm on the phone and will get …

Madison! What..."

•

"Dr. Pike, I'm here for a short time to provide some information that will explain a lot. As you study me, I appear as a hologram, that's all, and I arrived here in the light that touched down in Northfield – the very light that has commanded the attention of the world including yours here at the hospital. We did it on purpose to enable the world to experience more realities in quantum mechanics and relativity. I will not go into all of the detail now since the Dean and Dr. Treon discussed it with me a short time ago. They will explain it to you soon enough. What I came to do is answer some of your questions related to your field of study."

"The Dean and Dr. Treon?"

"Yes, and Sandra Lee, of course. The Dean and William have become friends. They are opposites in disciplines who enhance each other's work."

"We? You said we."

"Dr. Pike, there are so many of us, more than you can imagine who function as one. The deep seeded connection we all have is felt, recognized and shared. The other side of the light, Kay, that's where we find it and function as one."

"Madison, after you left I studied quantum mechanics and relativity. I went deep into noetics trying to find answers to understand everything you said to us."

"Dr. Pike, you can understand only so much while here on earth. Quantum mechanics is easy to explain up to a point. Everything I was and am is captured in a quark - three fermions - and three quarks which compromise a qubit. Consciousness, the key, is what I am today.

Relativity and the bending of time and space, that's how I travelled back and forth - through wormholes from one universe in a black hole to another universe in yet another black hole. It is real.

Noetics is the science of the intellect, consciousness, spirituality, thinking as you have discovered. How do we account for inner wisdom, direct knowing, and subjective understanding? Kay, we live in a universe of consciousness, a collective consciousness…a universal consciousness.

By now, you know that consciousness matters. Why else would a branch of metaphysical philosophy be concerned with the study of the mind as well as the intellect? The way you know you love your children, experiences you have had that cannot be explained or proven but feel real nevertheless, all fall under the discipline of noetics.

Does this remind you of William James? 'The truth that the present phenomenon of consciousness exits.' Remember, *The Will to Believe."*

"Madison, I'm at a loss for words. Why me? Why now? Why death? Why…"

"Better to ask, why the hospital? Why Reverend Anderson? Why the Dean and Dr. Treon? Why Dan?

Dan is easy. He was the key to getting us - you - into the Veterans Hospital to stop all that was going on there. Yes, I love him and left him with sweet memories he will experience again someday with another. The Dean, he was getting too far from reality and too far from the laity. He needed to engage himself in another discipline. Treon, his voice will be heard regarding relativity and quantum mechanics now that he is away from the ivory tower mentality. Nazeer, a reality check for all of us not having experienced Pakistan as she did and a catharsis for her in getting rid of those terrible memories. Rev. Anderson, he needed to learn to reach out to people, be accepting and non-judgmental rather than just preach. It happens to all of us - ego - as you well know.

And why the hospital, Dr. Pike? Remember the struggle you had with Victor Frankl's *Man's Search for Meaning?* 'Man cannot avoid suffering, but he can choose how to cope with it, find meaning in it.' It is one of the reasons you entered the fields of medicine and psychiatry after studying Frankl. 'Has all this suffering, this dying, a meaning? For a life whose meaning depends on whether one escapes suffering or not - happenstance - might not be worth living at all.' Frankl lost it all, Kay. He lost his parents, his wife, his unborn child, and his brother to the Holocaust. How does a person survive that? You and I are pikers when comparing our experience with pain to that kind of misery.

That thought continues to plague you, so you need to view it his way, Kay. I have been to the light. Life does have a meaning, a wonderful one at that. You discover it piece by piece each day and will in its entirety one day, as I have.

You also remember George Orwell's 1984. War is peace; freedom is slavery; ignorance is strength. Life seems that way, but truly it is not. But once again, if not always, we find ourselves fighting evil, another word created by man. The likes of Hitler, Stalin, Chavez, Escobar and so many more are the personification of evil. Is free will evil? Does it encourage evil? If we didn't have free will, would we have evil? And what about fate? Do we really have free will or is life just fate? These are tough questions that are answered in the light."

Imagine nothingness, Kay. You can't. But nothingness is real. It isn't hell; it's nothingness. The old boys had it right when they wrote 'Ashes to ashes; dust to dust.' Is that where those who are evil go rather than to the light? You tell me.

Refer to John Hick again, Kay. 'Death and suffering are not evils. They are how we come to know God.' *Evil and the Love of God*, what a good book that is."

"Death, Madison. What is death really?"

"Leo Tolstoy said 'What tells a man how he should live his life is the thought that he must die one day.'

Plato wrote in an *Apology* 'Death is one of two things - either death is a state of nothingness and utter unconsciousness, or as men say, there is a change and migration of the soul from this world to another.'

Even Hinduism claimed death is a natural event so that Atman can move nearer the release from rebirth. You remember, Kay, the Atman is reborn many times. But that doesn't answer your question, does it?

Let's go with Spinoza who said 'The wise person thinks nothing so little as death.' Then there is Plato who had a vital concern with death and constantly meditated on it.

Have you read *Close Encounters of the Cancer Kind*? Probably not, huh? Jeff Mason wrote 'Death and its concept are absolutely empty. No picture comes to mind. We must speak of death metaphorically. ...Death is real...Death is a blank wall...Death is not real; it is a door, portal, to another life.'

Kay, the framework for near-death experiences as reported by many cardiac arrest survivors was reported by Peter Dockrill in 2017. 'After clinical death occurred in rats, brain activity flared revealing electrical signature exceeding levels found in the animals waking states.'

Before I say look at me and ask the question about death again, Kay, you need to know scientists at the University of South Hampton spent 4 years examining more than 2000 people who experienced cardiac arrest in 15 hospitals across the U.K., U.S. and Australia. Forty percent described awareness when they were clinically dead and before their hearts were restarted. One even recounted the actions of the nursing staff. Kay, that was reported by Sarah Knapton of The Telegraph in 2014. You might remember reading it.

So, now all you need do is look at me, a hologram-like image, before asking the question regarding death again. Not only that, think about how we first met. I was the result of a near-death experience, so everyone thought. The possibility that my consciousness was captured in a quark, quarks or qubit would have been considered ridiculous if not crazy."

"Madison, what is next for you?"

"Remember what you asked Reverend Anderson, Kay? 'Is the light for later?" And remember the Einstein quote you used, 'A calm and modest life brings more happiness than the pursuit of success combined with constant restlessness.'

You know what is next for me."

Epilogue

One question still remains. "What happens when we die?" Does the answer lie with Nirvana, Atman, Heaven, Hell, the Noosphere, the Omega Point, or with Transhumanism? Is there an answer? Of course, we don't know. However, Madison's experience gives us a clue as to how we might get to where ever it is that we are going. If our mind, our consciousness, is found to be captured in waves or wavelets such as a fermions, quarks or qubits, then possibly, quite possibly, those waves or wavelets will take us to our final destination through a wormhole or an unknown like-entity that can travel to an ultimate destination in a picosecond or much faster.

Equally important is that death can be an adventure. Madison surely would record her death as an adventure - a great adventure, especially now. Like Madison, we can be full of life one day only to have it all change in a flash. If we were afraid of everything about which we did not know, we probably wouldn't go outside our home, look around a dark corner or make a difficult decision. However, she did move toward the conflict; she did take action in the midst of fear; she did pray but not just as a last resort. Madison also remembered the Apostle Paul who wrote in *I Corinthians* "We can only see through a glass, darkly. We don't know everything, but then [face to face] we will. God is like a magnificent and dread light that would extinguish any darkness approaching him."

Madison also taught us a most important lesson. That being, we may not have a choice but to keep our mind open to the improbable, maybe the impossible. We are all in this adventure, project humanity, together. We'll all be sure of that one day.

•

"In a real sense, all life is inter-related. All men are caught in an inescapable network of mutuality, tied in a single garment of destiny. Whatever affects one directly, affects all indirectly. I can never be what I ought to be until you are what you ought to be, and you can never be what you ought to be until I am what I ought to be…This is the inter-related structure of reality." Martin Luther King

•

"At the fundamental level, quantum mechanics tells us that it is impossible to predict accurately how a particle might behave in a given situation. One can, therefore, make predictions about the behavior of particles only on the basis of probability. If this is so…we cannot fully understand how the rest of the story unfolds." His Holiness, the Dalai Lama. *The Universe in a Single Atom*

INDEX

1.618	Page 140
631 CE	Page 62
666	Page 115
1984	Page 146
3760 BCE	Page 62
5778 CE	Page 62
6826	Page 115
A Farewell to Arms	Page 102
Alexithymia	Page 103
Alpha Centauri	Page 39
Andromeda	Pages 39, 54
Angels	Page 143
Angels & Demons	Page 56
Apology	Page 147
Apostle Paul	Epilogue, Page 77
Arrow of Time	Pages 131, 140
Athanasius	Page 70
Aquinas, Thomas	Pages 35, 36, 37, 38, 63, 66, 143
Atman	Epilogue, Pages 42, 111, 138, 147
Augustine	Pages 66, 127
Aurelius, Marcus	Page 74
Avesta	Page 86
Barbour, Ian	Pages 38, 69, 110, 132, 138
Balfour Declaration	Page 72
Bardo	Pages 32, 33, 51
Barth, Karl	Pages 63, 64
Beelzelbub	Page 127
Bible	Pages 69, 79, 110, 141, 146
Big Bang	Pages 22, 38, 53, 54, 77, 87, 103
Biocentrism	Pages 13, 69, 88
Black Hole	Pages 40, 54, 79, 109, 138, 139, 140
Book of Life	Page 141
Bosons	Prologue, Epilogue, Pages 13, 37, 42, 107
Brahma	Page 138
Bridge of the Separator	Pages 28, 86
Buber, Martin	Page 63
Buddhism	Pages 31, 33, 37, 39, 41, 42, 51, 62, 87
Calvin, John	Page 66
Categorical Principle	Page 25
Catholic	Pages 35, 74
CERN	Pages 55, 79, 107
Cesium	Page 124
Chandra X-ray Observatory	Page 128

China	Page 133
Chopra, Deepak	Pages 19, 20, 21, 101, 106
Chosen People	Page 141
City of God	Page 127
Classical Physics	Page 93
Close Encounters of the Cancer Kind	
	Page 147
Collected Dialogues by Plato	Pages 9, 89
Concerning Human Understanding	
	Page 142
Consciousness	Prologue, Epilogue, Pages 7,11, 19, 20, 84, 86, 88, 89, 90, 107, 110, 146
Confucius	Pages 62, 75
Copernicus	Page 54
1 Corinthians	Epilogue, Page 121
2 Corinthians	Page 77
Cosmic Shock Wave	Page 124
Council of Nicaea	Page 71
Covenant(s)	Page 142
Critique of Pure Reason	Page 68
CTE	Page 118
Dalai Lama	Epilogue, Pages 34, 35, 87, 89, 90, 141
Dark Energy	Pages 21, 55
Dark Matter	Page 21
Da Vinci	Page 140
Dead Sea Scrolls	Pages 105, 133, 136, 144
De Chardin	Pages 42, 65, 77, 86, 138
Descarte, Rene	Pages 91, 142
Devil	Page 116
Divine Proportion	Page 140
Dockrill, Peter	Page 147
DNA	Page 38
Durr, Hans Peter	Pages 17, 19, 77, 88
Earth	Page 11
Ecclesiastes	Page 77
Egypt	Page 140
Egyptian Book of the Dead	Page 74
Einstein	Prologue, Pages 21, 27, 37, 106, 120, 137, 148
Electromagnetic Field	Pages 13, 29, 60, 108
Energetic Cardiology	Pages 37, 38, 107
Energy	Page 108
Er	Page 89
Escobar, Pablo	Page 143
ESA	Pages 7, 29, 108
ESP	Page 17

Ethics	Page 91
Event Horizons	Page 139
Event Horizon Telescope	Pages 105, 107
Evil and the Love of God	Pages 66, 141, 147
Evolution	Page 111
Existence is Encounter	Page 64
Existential Theology	Page 63
Farewell to Arms	Page 102
Fate	Page 147
Fermions	Epilogue, Pages 13, 37, 42, 55, 107
Final Theory of God	Page 85
Four Known Forces of Nature	Pages 27, 87
FRB 121102	Pages 32, 40, 132
Free Will	Page 147
Frankl, Victor	Pages 143, 145, 146
GAIA Satellite	Page 60
Galaxy M87	Page 139
Gases	Page 22
Genesis	Pages 23, 140
Getting Used to Dying	Page 73
Gigalight Year	Page 131
Gnostic Gospels	Page 70
God	Page 138
God and the Afterlife	Page 82
God Particle	Page 55
Golden Rule	Page 75
Gospels	Page 69
Grand Design Theory	Page 20
Gravity	Page 61
Great Spirit	Page 138
Hadrons	Prologue
Hawking, Stephen	Pages 15, 23, 27, 30, 38, 44, 78, 79, 103, 104, 108, 139
Hawking Radiation	Pages 54, 140
Heaven	Epilogue, Pages 42, 110
Hell	Epilogue, Pages 41, 110
Hemingway, Ernest	Page 102
Hick, John	Pages 66, 141, 142, 147
Hitler	Page 143
Hinduism	Pages 31, 41
Hologram	Page 55
House of Song	Pages 42, 86
House of Druj	Page 86
Holy Spirit	Page 75
Hubble	Pages 24, 60, 106, 107, 127

Huxley, Julien	Pages 42, 44, 139
Isaiah	Page 110, 141
Islam	Pages 66, 86
Irenaeus of Lyons	Page 70
Jah/Hava	Page 62
James, William	Pages 90, 146
Jewish Apocrypha	Page 63
Jewish Spirituality	Page 66
Jawist	Page 23
Jesus	Pages 74, 109, 110, 137, 141
Jehovah	Page 138
Jung, Carl	Pages 14, 16, 17, 25, 67, 90
Juno	Page 109
Jupiter	Pages 58, 109
Kant, Immanuel	Pages 9, 14, 25, 68, 91
Karma	Page 87
Keillor, Garrison	Page 105
King, Martin Luther	Epilogue
Kierkegaard, Soren	Pages 64, 65, 97
Kilonova	Page 28
Knapton, Sarah	Page 148
Kushner, Rabbi Harry	Pages 66, 138
Lanza, Robert	Pages 13, 71, 88
Lao Tsu	Page 137
Leadership and the New Science	Page 132
Legion	Page 115
Lemaitre, Georges	Page 22
Leo	Page 31
Life Ever After	Page 83
Lightning Bolt	Page 127
Light Years	Pages 23, 29, 39
Locke, John	Page 142
Long, Jeffrey	Page 83
Loop Quantum Gravity	Pages 61, 139
LSD	Pages 25, 32
Luke	Page 127
Luther, Martin	Page 66
Machiavellian Intelligence Hypothesis	Page 103
Mahayana Sutras	Page 33
Mans Search for Meaning	Page 145
Maret, Karl H.	Page 38
Mars	Page 108
Mary	Pages 76, 109, 137

Mason, Jeff	Page 147
Matter/Mass	Page 44
McLaren, Brian	Pages 42, 90
McMillan, J.B.	Pages 25, 42, 85
Meditations	Page 74
Microgravity	Page 142
Microlensing	Page 128
Mitzrayim	Page 140
Milky Way	Pages 11, 29, 39, 108, 109
Mind/Body Dualism	Page 90
Mirror Universe	Pages 132, 139, 140
Mitchell, Edgar	Page 16
Mohammed	Pages 62, 141
Moody, Moody	Page 83
Moon	Page 40
Morse, Melvin	Page 97
Moses	Pages 23, 42, 76, 110, 141
Mt. Hermon	Pages 76, 109, 110, 141
Mt. Sinai	Page 142
Multiverse	Pages 20, 108
Muon	Pages 56, 129, 130, 131
Myers-Briggs	Pages 17, 110
n-Body Problem	Page 132
Namaste	Page 41
Near Death Experiences	Pages 6, 49, 75 81, 82, 147
Neidermeyer, Doug	Page 23
Niebuhr, Reinhold	Page 65
Neutrinos	Page 79
Nirvana	Epilogue, Page 41
Noetics	Pages 145, 146
Noosphere	Epilogue, Pages 86, 138
North Star Mutual	Page 61
Nothingness	Page 147
Old Testament	Pages 23, 110, 142
Omega Centauri	Page 39
Omega Point	Epilogue, Pages 42, 86, 138
Orear	Page 38
Orwell, George	Pages 143, 146
Out-of-body	Pages 6, 14
Pachomian Monks	Page 70
Pearsall	Page 38
Phenomenon of Man	Page 86
Phi	Page 140
Philippians	Page 141
Photon Teleportation	Page 133

Physics, Classical	Page 93
Physics, Quantum	Pages 36, 93
Physics, Relativistic	Page 15
Physics, Theoretical	Pages 21, 71, 93
Picosecond	Prologue, Epilogue, Pages 23, 127, 128
Planet Gliese 832c	Pages 24, 39
Planet K2 – 18b	Page 31
Planet OGLE	Page 58
Plato	Pages 9, 42, 89, 90, 147
Pluto	Page 40
Priestly Story	Page 23
Promised Land	Page 42
Property/Mind Dualism	Page 90
Proton	Prologue
Ptolemy	Page 54
Pyramids	Page 129
Quanta	Pages 11, 13
Quantum Bits	Pages 11, 141, 148
Quantum Entanglement	Page 36
Quantum Fluctuation	Pages 22, 39, 61
Quantum Mechanics	Prologue, Pages 36, 77, 83, 122, 145
Quantum Teleportation	Page 133
Quark	Prologue, Epilogue, Pages 37, 93, 97, 121, 141, 147
Qumran	Pages 105, 136
Rein	Page 38
Relationships in Recovery	Page 128
Relativity	Prologue, Pages 15, 27, 145
Revelations	Page 141
Republic	Page 89
Romans 5	Pages 15, 32
Rovelli, Carlo	Pages 7, 19, 23, 30, 36, 38, 44, 61, 79, 108, 139
Russek	Page 38
Sagittarius	Pages 28, 29
Salvation	Page 110
Satellites	Page 122
Satellites, Communication	Page 127
Satellites, GPS	Page 127
Savior	Page 41
Schwartz	Page 38
Scorpio	Pages 28, 29
Seven Brief Lessons on Physics	Prologue, Pages 7, 36, 60
Seven Spiritual Laws of Success	Page 106
Seventh Day Adventists	Page 74

Singularity	Pages 87, 140
Siraat	Page 86
Six Day War	Page 72
Socrates	Pages 9, 10, 89
South Hampton, U of	Page 147
Space	Pages 15, 60, 127
Space Junk	Page 122
Speed of Light	Pages 93, 122, 127, 131
Spinoza, Baruch	Pages 73, 91, 138, 142, 147
Spitzer Telescope	Pages 104, 105, 107
Stalin	Page 143
Static Universe	Page 106
Steinbeck, John	Page 53
Stockholm syndrome	Page 77
Stress	Page 33
Subconscious Mind	Page 25
Summa Theologica	Pages 35, 143
Sun	Pages 19, 60
Sun God	Page 74
Superstring Theory	Page 30
Synchronous Rotation	Page 40
Tao	Pages 137, 140
Tao Te Ching	Page 137
Telegraph	Page 148
Theory of Neo-Biocentrism	Page 71
Tononi, Giulio	Page 7
Thermodynamics	Page 19
Thales of Miletus	Page 20
Thin Place	Pages 76, 109, 137
Tibetan Book of the Dead	Page 33
Tittel, Wolfgang	Page 93
Tolstoy, Leo	Page 147
Transfiguration	Page 12
Transhumanism	Epilogue, Pages 42, 44, 139
Tripitaka	Page 33
Universe in a Single Atom	Pages 87, 121
University of Calgary	Page 93
Upanishads	Page 41
Vedas	Page 41
Virgo	Page 139
WCCO	Pages 104, 118
Will to Believe	Pages 90, 146
Webb, James, Telescope	Pages 104, 107
Wheatley, Margaret J.	Page 132

Wormhole	Pages 52, 53, 93, 132, 133, 145
Yeshua	Page 138
Zhang Xianliang	Page 73
Zoroaster	Pages 42, 86
Zoroastrianism	Page 86